First World War
and Army of Occupation
War Diary
France, Belgium and Germany

3 CAVALRY DIVISION
Headquarters, Branches and Services
General Staff Appendices to 1141
5 August 1918 - 21 December 1918

WO95/1142/6

The Naval & Military Press Ltd
www.nmarchive.com
Published in association with The National Archives

Published by

The Naval & Military Press Ltd

Unit 10 Ridgewood Industrial Park,

Uckfield, East Sussex,

TN22 5QE England

Tel: +44 (0) 1825 749494

www.naval-military-press.com

www.nmarchive.com

This diary has been reprinted in facsimile from the original. Any imperfections are inevitably reproduced and the quality may fall short of modern type and cartographic standards.

© **Crown Copyright**
Images reproduced by permission of The National Archives, London, England, 2015.

Contents

Document type	Place/Title	Date From	Date To
Heading	War Diary of General Staff 3rd Cavalry Division Intelligence Summary August 1918		
Miscellaneous	Cover For Documents. Nature Of Enclosures.		
Operation(al) Order(s)	3rd Cavalry Division Order No.38.	05/08/1918	05/08/1918
Miscellaneous	Preliminary Instructions & Information.	05/08/1918	05/08/1918
Operation(al) Order(s)	3rd Cavalry Division Order No.39.	06/08/1918	06/08/1918
Miscellaneous	March Table "A" Issued With 3rd Cav. Div.Order 39.		
Miscellaneous	Table "B" Issued With 3rd Cav. Order No.39.		
Operation(al) Order(s)	3rd Cavalry Division Order No.40.	06/08/1918	06/08/1918
Miscellaneous	Addenda to Preliminary Instructions & Information.	06/08/1918	06/08/1918
Operation(al) Order(s)	3rd Cavalry Division Order No.41.	07/08/1918	07/08/1918
Miscellaneous	March Table Issued With 3rd Cavalry Division Order No.41.		
Miscellaneous	A Form Messages And Signals		
Miscellaneous	6th Cavalry Brigade.		
Miscellaneous	A Form Messages And Signals		
Miscellaneous	6th Cav. Bde.		
Miscellaneous	A Form Messages And Signals		
Operation(al) Order(s)	3rd Cavalry Division Order No.42.	15/08/1918	15/08/1918
Miscellaneous	March Table Issued With 3rd Cavalry Division Order No.42.		
Miscellaneous	A Form Messages And Signals		
Operation(al) Order(s)	3rd Cavalry Division Order No.44.	21/08/1918	21/08/1918
Miscellaneous	March Table Issued With 3rd Cavalry Division Order No.44		
Operation(al) Order(s)	3rd Cavalry Division Order No.45.	25/08/1918	25/08/1918
Miscellaneous	March Table Issued With 3rd Cavalry Division Order No.45.		
Operation(al) Order(s)	3rd Cavalry Division Order No.46.	26/08/1918	26/08/1918
Miscellaneous	A Form Messages And Signals		
Heading	War Diary of General Staff 3rd Cavalry Division Intelligence Summary September 1918		
Miscellaneous	Cover For Documents. Nature Of Enclosures.		
Miscellaneous	Report On The Operations East Of Arras In Which The 10th (P.W.O) Royal Hussars Took Part	02/09/1918	02/09/1918
Miscellaneous	Reference Map, Sheet Lens 11, 1/100,000	09/09/1918	09/09/1918
Operation(al) Order(s)	3rd Cavalry Division Order No.50.	14/09/1918	14/09/1918
Miscellaneous	March Table Issued With 3rd Cavalry Division Order No.50.		
Operation(al) Order(s)	3rd Cavalry Division Order No.53	17/09/1918	17/09/1918
Miscellaneous	Special Instructions For Cavalry Manoeuvres	16/09/1918	16/09/1918
Miscellaneous	A Form Messages And Signals		
Miscellaneous	A Form. Messages And Signals.	17/09/1918	17/09/1918
Miscellaneous	3rd Cav. Div. G.0.10		
Operation(al) Order(s)	3rd Cavalry Division Order No.54.	18/09/1918	18/09/1918
Operation(al) Order(s)	3rd Cavalry Division Order No.55.	24/09/1918	24/09/1918
Miscellaneous	March Table Issued With 3rd Cavalry Division Order No.55.		
Operation(al) Order(s)	3rd Cavalry Division Order No.56.	20/09/1918	20/09/1918

Type	Description	Date From	Date To
Miscellaneous	March Table Issued With 3rd Cavalry Division Order No.56.		
Operation(al) Order(s)	3rd Cavalry Division Order No.57.	27/09/1918	27/09/1918
Miscellaneous	March Table Issued With 3rd Cavalry Division Order No.57.		
Miscellaneous	A Form Messages And Signals		
Miscellaneous	3rd Cavalry Division Order No.58.	30/09/1918	30/09/1918
Miscellaneous	A Form Messages And Signals		
Miscellaneous	Cover For Documents. Nature Of Enclosures.		
Heading	War Diary of General Staff 3rd Cavalry Division October 1918		
Heading	War Diary of General Staff Cavalry Division Intelligence Summary October 1918		
Operation(al) Order(s)	3rd Cavalry Division Order No.59.	01/10/1918	01/10/1918
Miscellaneous	A Form Messages And Signals		
Operation(al) Order(s)	3rd Cavalry Division Order No.61.	02/10/1918	02/10/1918
Miscellaneous	A Form Messages And Signals		
Operation(al) Order(s)	3rd. Cavalry Division Order No.62.	02/10/1918	02/10/1918
Miscellaneous	A Form Messages And Signals		
Operation(al) Order(s)	3rd Cavalry Division Order No.63.	05/10/1918	05/10/1918
Operation(al) Order(s)	3rd Cavalry Division Order No.64.	06/10/1918	06/10/1918
Operation(al) Order(s)	3rd Cavalry Division Order No.65.	06/10/1918	06/10/1918
Operation(al) Order(s)	3rd Cavalry Division Order No.66.	07/10/1918	07/10/1918
Miscellaneous	March Table Issued With 3rd Cavalry Division Order No.66.		
Miscellaneous	Addenda to 3rd Cavalry Division Order No.64.	07/10/1918	07/10/1918
Miscellaneous	A Form Messages And Signals		
Operation(al) Order(s)	3rd Cavalry Division Order No.70.	09/10/1918	09/10/1918
Miscellaneous	A Form Messages And Signals		
Operation(al) Order(s)	3rd Cavalry Division Order No.71.	10/10/1918	10/10/1918
Miscellaneous	A Form Messages And Signals		
Operation(al) Order(s)	3rd Cavalry Division Order No.72.	11/10/1918	11/10/1918
Miscellaneous	A Form Messages And Signals		
Operation(al) Order(s)	3rd Cavalry Division Order No.73.	13/10/1918	13/10/1918
Operation(al) Order(s)	3rd Cavalry Division Order No.74.	13/10/1918	13/10/1918
Miscellaneous	March Table With 3rd Cavalry Division Order No.64		
Operation(al) Order(s)	3rd Cavalry Division Order No.75.	14/10/1918	14/10/1918
Heading	War Diary of General Staff 3rd Cavalry Division Intelligence Summaries November 1918.		
Operation(al) Order(s)	3rd Cavalry Division Order No.76.	06/11/1918	06/11/1918
Miscellaneous	To All Recipients Of 3rd Cavalry Division Order No.77.	06/11/1918	06/11/1918
Operation(al) Order(s)	3rd Cavalry Division Order No.77.	06/11/1918	06/11/1918
Miscellaneous	March Table Issued With 3rd Cavalry Division Order No.77.		
Miscellaneous	Reference Maps 1/100,000, Valenciennes And Tournai	08/11/1918	08/11/1918
Operation(al) Order(s)	3rd Cavalry Division Order No.78.	08/11/1918	08/11/1918
Miscellaneous	Second G.446	08/11/1918	08/11/1918
Operation(al) Order(s)	3rd Cavalry Division Order No.79.	10/11/1918	10/11/1918
Operation(al) Order(s)	3rd Cavalry Division Order No.80.	11/11/1918	11/11/1918
Miscellaneous	A Form Messages And Signals		
Operation(al) Order(s)	3rd Cavalry Division Order No.81	12/11/1918	12/11/1918
Miscellaneous		11/11/1918	11/11/1918
Operation(al) Order(s)	3rd Cavalry Division Order No.82.	15/11/1918	15/11/1918
Miscellaneous	March Table Issued With 3rd Cavalry Division Order No.82		

Miscellaneous	Reference 3rd Cavalry Division Order No.83.	17/11/1918	17/11/1918
Operation(al) Order(s)	3rd Cavalry Division Order No.83.	16/11/1918	16/11/1918
Miscellaneous	March Order Issued With 3rd Cavalry Division Order No.83.		
Operation(al) Order(s)	3rd Cavalry Division Order No.84.	19/11/1918	19/11/1918
Miscellaneous	March Table Issued With 3rd Cavalry Division Order No.84.		
Operation(al) Order(s)	3rd Cavalry Division Order No.85.	20/11/1918	20/11/1918
Miscellaneous	March Table Issued With 3rd Cavalry Division Order No.85.		
Operation(al) Order(s)	3rd Cavalry Division Order No.86.	23/11/1918	23/11/1918
Operation(al) Order(s)	3rd Cavalry Division Order No.87.	30/11/1918	30/11/1918
Heading	War Diary of General Staff 3rd Cavalry Division Intelligence December 1918		
Miscellaneous	Appendix 1	05/12/1918	05/12/1918
Miscellaneous	A Form Messages And Signals		
Miscellaneous	Appendix 2	07/12/1918	07/12/1918
Operation(al) Order(s)	3rd Cavalry Division Order No.88.	09/12/1918	09/12/1918
Operation(al) Order(s)	3rd Cavalry Division Order No.89.	12/12/1918	12/12/1918
Miscellaneous	March Table "A" Issued With 3rd Cavalry Division Order No. 89.		
Miscellaneous	Amendment To 3rd Cavalry Division Order No.89.	14/12/1918	14/12/1918
Miscellaneous	Amendment No.1 To 3rd Cavalry Division Order No.89.	12/12/1918	12/12/1918
Miscellaneous	Amended March Table "A" Issued With 3rd Cav. Div. Order No.89.		
Miscellaneous	G.S. 248/97 Appendix 7	21/12/1918	21/12/1918
Miscellaneous	3rd Cavalry Division Order No. 42	15/08/1918	15/08/1918

CONFIDENTIAL

War Diary
of
General Staff
3rd Cavalry Division
Intelligence Summaries
August, 1918

(6339) Wt. W160/M3016 1,500,000 10/17 McA & W Ltd (E 1898) Forms W3091.   Army Form W.3091.

Cover for Documents.

Nature of Enclosures.

Notes, or Letters written.

Appendix 1

SECRET.

Copy No.....

3rd Cavalry Division Order No. 38.

5th August, 1918.

Ref. Map 1/100,000 AMIENS Sheet, & 1/40,000 62E.

1. The 4th Brigade R.H.A. at present in Mobile Reserve in III Corps Area will rejoin the 3rd Cavalry Division in area west and south-west of AMIENS, marching by day on August 6th and clearing present area by 12-noon.

2. (a) Move will take place under orders of C.R.H.A. but on arrival in new area C. & K Batteries and R.C.H.A. Brigade will rejoin 6th, 7th and Canadian Cavalry Brigades respectively, who will arrive in the area during night 6/7th.

   (b) Route: BEAUCOURT – ALLONVILLE–AMIENS Switch.

   (c) Destination. H.Q. 4th Brigade R.H.A. and Divl. Ammunition Column to PONT DE METZ area.
   C. Battery R.H.A. to RENANCOURT area.
   K. Battery R.H.A. to MONTIERES area.
   R.C.H.A. Brigade to Gardens just west of AMIENS in R.3.d. and R.4.c.

3. Following distances will be observed.

   Between Sections 500 yards.
   Between Sections of Amm. Col. 500 yards.
   Between Batteries 1,000 yards.

4. Billeting parties will meet Staff Captains or their representatives as under tomorrow, August 6th.

   H.Q. 4th Brigade R.H.A. & D.A.C. to meet Camp Commandant at PONT DE METZ Church at 10-0.am.

   C. Battery RENANCOURT Church 10-0.am.
   K. Battery MONTIERES Church 10-0.am.

   R.C.H.A. Brigade at Road junction R.4.d.0.5. at 9-0.am.

5. 3rd Cavalry Division will administer the 4th Bde.R.H.A. from 7th August inclusive.

6. ACKNOWLEDGE.

S.S. Howls, Major
for Lieut-Colonel,
General Staff, 3rd Cavalry Division.

Issued at 9 p.m.

Copies to:- 1. 6th Cav Bde.
2. 7th Cav Bde.
3. Candn.Cav.Bde.
4. C.R.H.A.
5. 3rd Signal Sqdn.
6. S.A.A.Section D.A.C.
7. A.D.M.S.

SECRET.

G.X.200/3
5.8.18.

PRELIMINARY INSTRUCTIONS & INFORMATION. App 2

1. The object of the operation to be carried out by the Fourth Army is to relieve the pressure on AMIENS.

Formations attacking.

2. (a) The Canadian Corps will attack the enemy's position between the AMIENS-ROYE Road and the VILLERS BRETONNEUX - CHAULNES Railway (both inclusive) at an hour and date to be notified later.

(b) The XXXI French Corps will be attacking on the right of the Canadian Corps.

(c) The Australian Corps will be attacking on the left of the Canadian Corps.

Allotment of Troops.

3. The attack of the Canadian Corps will be carried out by the 3rd Canadian Division on the right, 1st Canadian Division in the Centre, and 2nd Canadian Division on the Left.
The 4th Canadian Division will be in Reserve.
A Battalion of Mark V Tanks will be attached to each Canadian Division.
The 3rd Cavalry Division with 1 Battalion (48) Whippet Tanks attacked will be operating in Canadian Corps area with a special mission.
An independent force (2 Canadian Motor Machine Gun Brigades, 1 Canadian Cyclist Battalion, and 1 Section 6" Newton Mortars) has also been allotted a special task.

Objectives, Boundaries, etc.

4. Objectives, Corps and Divisional Boundaries are as shewn on Maps issued today at Divisional Conference.

Surprise & Secrecy.

5. The attack will be a surprise attack, without preliminary bombardment, under cover of Artillery Barrage.
It is therefore of vital importance that secrecy be observed.
All movement of troops and transport will take place by night bith in forward and back areas. No troops will be on the march except between the hours of 9.0 p.m. and 3.45 a.m. By 4.0 a.m. all troops and transport must be clear of roads and under cover.
Special arrangements are necessary to ensure that no movement is seen by enemy aircraft. Each Squadron or similar unit will detail an Officer whose duty will be to see that personnel, horses and vehicles remain under cover from hostile aircraft during daylight.
Reconnoitring Officers must not go about in parties larger than two persons, must avoid high ground and O.P's, and must not display maps in the forward area.

Tasks.

6. (a) The task of 1, 2, 3, Canadian Divisions on the first day is to capture and hold the RED Line except on left of 2nd Canadian Division where the task includes the capture and holding of the BLUE Line.

(b) The task of the 3rd Cavalry Division with 1 Battalion Whippet Tanks (of 3rd Tank Brigade) attached, is to follow up the Canadian Divisions advance to the RED Line, pass through the Infantry and capture and hold the BLUE Dotted Line, Northwards from ROYE Road; they will also exploit their success East of BLUE Dotted Line and S. and S.E. of ROYE Road.

......(c)

(c) The 1st Cavalry Division will be following 3rd Cavalry Division with one Brigade following leading Brigade of 3rd Cavalry Division.

(d) The 4th Canadian Division will follow the 1st and 3rd Canadian Divisions, passing through them on the RED Line and relieving the Cavalry in or assisting them to capture BLUE Dotted Line.

(e) The Independent Force will pass through the 3rd Canadian Division and make good the line of the ROYE Road between the RED Line and BLUE Dotted Line forming a flank to 3rd Cavalry Division towards the South. As the fight progresses, this force will continue to exploit success down the ROYE Road acting as a link between the most advanced Cavalry and the leading Infantry.

Artillery.
7. Barrage starts at Zero 200 yards beyond Infantry jumping off line.
A protective barrage will be maintained in front of GREEN Line till Zero plus 4 hours, after which all Field Artillery Barrages will cease.
One Brigade of Field Artillery has been detailed to follow in close support of each Canadian Division.

Cavalry Assembly Areas.
8. Areas of assembly for Cavalry are as shewn on the Map issued at the Divisional Conference today.

Track.
Cavalry Track is also shewn on this map and will be marked by white flags at trench crossings and with arrows and Divisional signs at intervals.

Flares, S.O.S. &c.
9. Lights Signals used by Canadian Corps are shewn in Appendix "A" attached.
The Cavalry Corps Signal will be used as laid down, to mark position occupied.
Should a S.O.S. Signal be necessary, that in force for the Canadian Corps will be used. A supply of these is being arranged for and will be issued to Brigades.

Tanks.
10. Notes on the employment of the Whippet Tanks with Cavalry are issued herewith.- Appendix "B".

Maps.
11. Every Officer must be in possesion of AMIENS Map Sheet 1/100,000.

Issued at 9 a.m.
5th August, 1918.

(Sd) G.P.COSENS,
Lieut.Colonel,
General Staff, 3rd Cavalry Division.

Copies to:-   6th Cavalry Brigade.   x
               7th Cavalry Brigade.   x
               Canadian Cavalry Brigade. x
               3rd Field Squadron.   x
               3rd Signal Squadron.   x
               C.R.H.A.   x
               "Q".
               A.D.M.S.
               A.P.M.
               Fourth Army.
               Cavalry Corps.
               Canadian Corps.

x With 2 Maps.

App 3

SECRET.   Copy No. 23

3rd Cavalry Division Order No. 39.

6th August, 1918.

Ref. Map 1/40,000 62E. and 57E.

1. 3rd Cavalry Division, less B. Echelons, Heavy Sections Cavalry Field Ambulances and Heavy Section 3rd Cav. Reserve Park will move to a concentration area west and south-west of AMIENS during night August 6/7th in accordance with March Table A attached.

    4th Brigade R.H.A. and R.C.H.A. Brigade and Divisional Amm: Column will move into concentration area as above on August 6th under orders that have been issued separately.

    R.C.H.A. Brigade, C. and K Batteries will come under the orders of Canadian, 6th and 7th Cavalry Brigades respectively so soon as Brigades arrive in concentration area.

2. B. Echelon Divisional H.Q., B. Echelons of Brigades accompanied by Heavy Sections of their affiliated Field Ambulances, and Heavy Section 3rd Cavalry Reserve Park will be concentrated on August 7th at HANGEST-sur-SOMME in accordance with March Table B attached, and will come under the orders of Captain W.H. JENKINS, 7th Dragoon Gds. who will make his Headquarters at present Canadian Cavalry Brigade Headquarters.

    Billeting parties will meet Captain Jenkins at Canadian Cavalry Brigade old Headquarters, HANGEST, at 8-0.am. August 7th.

3. Following distances will be maintained by all troops marching under Table "A".

    50 yards between Regiments.
    20 yards between Squadrons and similar units.

    For troops marching under Table "B".

    1,000 yards between groups of 6 vehicles.

4. 3rd Cavalry Division Report Centre will close at YZEUX at 9-0.pm. August 6th and re-open at PONT DE METZ same hour.

5. ACKNOWLEDGE.

Lieut-Colonel,
General Staff, 3rd Cavalry Division.

Issued at 7 A.M.

Copies to:-
1. 6th Cav Bde.
2. 7th Cav Bde.
3. Candn.Cav Bde.
4. C.R.H.A.
5. 3rd Sig.Sqdn.
6. 3rd Fd.Sqdn.
7. Aux.H.T.Coy.
8. 3rd Cav.Res.Park.
9. S.A.A.Sect.D.A.C.
10. Camp Commdt.
11. O.C.A.S.C.
12. A.D.M.S.
13. A.D.V.S.
17. D.M.G.O.
18. Cavalry Corps.
19. Canadian Corps.
20. Fourth Army.
21-23. War Diary.
24-26. File.

MARCH TABLE "A" Issued with 3rd Cav.Div.Order 39.

Serial No.	Date.	Unit.	From	To	Starting Point.	Route.	Remarks.
1.	Aug. 5th	Candn. Cav. Brigade.	HANGEST - SOUES Area.	AMIENS Gardons R.3d. - R.4c -R.9a.	X Roads I.6.d.5.9.	Road junction J.8.d: FOURDRINOY - X Rds.J.23.A. - FERRIERES-SAVEUSE.	Head tp pass S.P. 9-30.pm. Not to enter FERRIERES before 11-30.pm. & column to clear that place by 1-30.a.m.
2.	6th.	6th Cavalry Brigade.	LE MESGE - RIENCOURT Area.	RENANCOURT Area.	Western exit CAVILLON.	X Roads J.23.a. - Road FERRIERES - Road junction Q.9.d.2.9. - PONT DE METZ.	Not to enter FOURDRINOY before 11-30.pm.
3.	6th.	Divl. H.Q. H.Q. & A.S.C. 3rd Sig.Sqdn.	YZEUX.	PONT DE METZ.	Any.	PICQUIGNY - MONTIERES - R.3.b - RENANCOURT.	Head to enter PICQUIGNY at 11-30.pm.
4.	6th.	3rd Fd.Sqdn.	BETHENCOURT ST.OUEN.	PONT DE METZ.	Road junction V.27.c.	BELLOY - PICQUIGNY - AILLY - MONTIERES R.3.b. - RENANCOURT.	Head to pass S.P. 10.pm. to clear PICQUIGNY by 12. midnight.
5.	6th.	Aux.H.T.Coy. S.A.A.Sect.of D.A.C.	BETHENCOURT ST.OUEN.	PONT DE METZ.	Road junction V.27.c.	--do--	Head to pass S.P 10.pm. & to clear PICQUIGNY 12-15.a.m.
6.	6th.	7th Cavalry Brigade.	BOURDON.	MONTIERES Area.	Any.	HANGEST - CROIX - PICQUIGNY.	Not to enter HANGEST before 11-15.pm.and to be in bivouac by 3-45.am.
7.	7th.	Light Section 3rd Cav.Res. Park.	BETHENCOURT ST.OUEN.	PONT DE METZ.	Any.	BELLOY - PICQUIGNY - FERRIERES.	Not to leave camp before 9-0.p.m. & to be in bivouac by 3-45.am.

TABLE "B" P.T.O.

TABLE "B" Issued with 3rd Cav. Order No. 39.

Serial No.	Date.	Unit.	From.	To.	Route.	Remarks.
1.	Aug. 7th.	B.Echelon 6th Cav.Bde. } Heavy Section 6th C.F.A. }	LE MESGE Aron.	HANGEST.	Any.	To enter HANGEST at 10-0.am.
2.	7th.	B.Echelon 7th Cav.Bde. } Heavy Section 7th C.F.A. }	BOURDON.	HANGEST.	Any.	To enter HANGEST at 9-0.am.
3.	7th.	B.Echelon of Divl.H.Q. } H.Q. A.S.C. }	YZEUX.	HANGEST.	Any.	To enter HANGEST at 11-0.am.
4.	7th.	Heavy Section 3rd Cav.Res. Park.	BETHENCOURT ST. OUEN.	HANGEST.	BOURDON.	Not to enter HANGEST before 12-noon.

-2-

4. The Canadian Cavalry Brigade will keep in close touch with the Infantry Advance of 1st and 3rd Canadian Divisions by means of patrols and will also detail patrols to reconnoitre crossings over the River LUCE from DEMUIN to CAIX, both inclusive, reporting on their suitability for Tanks and Cavalry.

5. On crossing the River LUCE the Division will move forward on a two Brigade frontage, Canadian Cavalry Brigade on the right (South) and 7th Cavalry Brigade on the left (North).
Objective will be BLUE DOTTED Line from ROYE - AMIENS Road to E.16.c.7.0.
First Bound: a line running from D.29.central to E.7. central.
Dividing line between Brigades: K.3.a.1.4. - E.26.central - E.19.central - D.11.central.
The Canadian Cavalry Brigade will gain touch with Canadian Motor Machine Gun Brigade along the ROYE Road and the 7th Cavalry Brigade with the 1st Cavalry Division on their left.
The 6th Cavalry Brigade and 16 Tanks will be in Divisional Support.

6. If the crossings over the River LUCE are impracticable for Tanks, the Canadian Cavalry Brigade and 7th Cavalry Brigade with the Battalion of Tanks will move north of River LUCE via CAIX.
Role for Canadian Cavalry Brigade and Tanks will be to mop up enemy in the quadrilateral CAIX - CAYEUX - BEAUCOURT - LE QUESNEL, prior to seizing objective.
Role for 7th Cavalry Brigade will be to support Canadian Cavalry Brigade if required and to form a flank to the east on the objective, until the Canadian Cavalry Brigade have completed the mopping up, when Canadian Cavalry Brigade will seize their objective.
6th Cavalry Brigade will be in Divisional Support.

7. A.1 Echelons will march Divisionalized from Assembly Area in rear of 3rd Field Squadron (see para. 3) under Captain de TRAFFORD, Royal Dragoons.
D.A.C. and Aux.H.T.Company will remain in Assembly Area until ordered forward.
A.2 Echelons will be Divisionalized under Major C.GOODDAY, L.S.H. at PONT DE METZ, and will march to an Assembly position north of BOVES. Time and route to be notified later. Cyclists will move with the A.2 Echelon.
Light Section Reserve Park will remain in PONT DE METZ Area and await orders.

8. Mobile Veterinary Sections will be Divisionalized at PONT DE METZ by 4.pm. Y day and will come under orders of A.D.V.S.
During operations 13th M.V.S. will be at Railhead, SALEUX.
14th M.V.S. and "A" Canadian M.V.S. will proceed to BOVES under A.D.V.S's. orders. "A" Canadian M.V.S. will move to N.W. edge of BOIS DE GENTELLES at Zero plus 4 hours.

9. Medical arrangements will be notified later.

10. Divisional Report Centre will be located as follows :-

At Zero hour. T.3.b.2.4. X Roads and Track.
At Zero plus 4 hours. N. end of CACHY. U.2.d.9.9.
At Zero plus 4½ hours. V.7.c.0.5. N. end of MORGEMONT WOOD.

11.
P.T.O.

11.   Orders for the move from the area W. and S.W. of AMIENS to the Assembly area will be issued later.

12.   Acknowledge by wire.

[signature]

Lieut-Colonel,
General Staff, 3rd Cavalry Division.

Issued at 9-0.am.

Copies to :-
1. 6th Cavalry Brigade.
2. 7th   "   "
3. Candn. "   "
4. 3rd Signal Sqdn.
5. 3rd Field Sqdn.
6. C.R.H.A.
7. "Q".
8. D.A.C.
9. A.D.M.S.
10. A.D.V.S.
11. A.P.M.
12. O.C.A.S.C.
13. 3rd Cav. Res. Park.
14. Camp Comndt.
15. D.M.G.O.
16. D.G.O.
17. Canadian Corps.   (for information)
18. 1st Canadian Div.
19. 2nd   "   "
20. 3rd   "   "
21. 4th   "   "
22. Cavalry Corps.   (for information)
23. 1st Cavalry Division.
24. 2nd Cavalry Division.
25. G.O.C.,3rd Tank Brigade.
26. O.C. 3rd (Light) Tank Battalion.
27. Fourth Army.   (for information)
28. No. 6 Squadron R.A.F. (for information)
29. Australian Corps.   (for information)
30. Major GOODDAY, L.S.H.
31. Capt. De TRAFFORD, Royal Dragoons.
32 - 34. War Diary.
35 - 44. File.

SECRET.   Copy No.....

3rd Cavalry Division Order No. 40.

6th August, 1918.

Reference 1/40,000 Sheets 62D and 66E.

1. (a) The Fourth Army will attack the enemy's positions between MORLANCOURT and the AMIENS - ROYE Road (inclusive) on a date to be notified later. The 1st French Army will co-operate with an attack on the enemy's positions between the AMIENS - ROYE Road (exclusive) and the AVRE Valley.

   (b) The objectives and boundaries between Corps, and Divisions in the case of the Canadian Corps, and between the Fourth Army and the 1st French Army, are shown on map issued at Divisional Conference.

   (c) The troops which will carry out this attack are as follows :-

   III Corps with 10th Tank Battalion attached.
   Australian Corps with 5th Tank Brigade attached.
   Canadian Corps with 4th Tank Brigade attached.
   Cavalry Corps with 3rd Tank Brigade attached.

   The 9th Tank Battalion will be in Army Reserve.

   (d) At the outset of the operations, the 3rd Cavalry Division will work under the Canadian Corps. It will revert to the command of the Cavalry Corps as soon as the whole of the RED Line on the Canadian Corps front has been reached by the Infantry.

2. The task of the 3rd Cavalry Division with 1 Bn. Whippet Tanks is to follow up the advance of the 1st and 3rd Canadian Divisions, and of the 1st Cavalry Division with 1 Bn. Whippet Tanks to follow up the 2nd Canadian Division to the RED Line, where the Cavalry will pass through the Infantry and proceed to capture and hold the BLUE DOTTED Line, northwards from the ROYE Road to Railway, at the same time exploiting their success east of the BLUE DOTTED Line and south and south-east of the ROYE Road.

3. In consequence, the 3rd Cavalry Division will be ready to move on Zero Day, from the assembly area about N.32 and T.2 (shown on map issued   ) along the Cavalry Track.
   Order of March :-

   Canadian Cavalry Brigade.
   One Brigade of 1st Cavalry Division.
   7th Cavalry Brigade.
   6th Cavalry Brigade.
   Field Squadron (after completion of Special Mission).

   Batteries R.H.A. and R.C.H.A. Brigade will accompany Brigades.

   Two Companies of Whippet Tanks, 16 in each Company, will move with Canadian Cavalry Brigade and one Company with 6th Cavalry Brigade in support.

SECRET. Copy No...

ADDENDA to PRELIMINARY INSTRUCTIONS & INFORMATION.

6th August, 1918.

(TO BE BURNT BEFORE LEAVING AMIENS - PONT DE METZ Area)

Ref. 1/40,000 Sheets 62D & 66E.

1. In continuation of GX.200/3 dated August 5th, the following is issued for information and guidance of all concerned.

2. Role of the 4th Canadian Division.
The task of the 4th Canadian Division is to advance at Zero following the 1st and 3rd Canadian Divisions, pass through them on the RED Line and relieve the Cavalry in, or assist them in capturing, the BLUE DOTTED Line between the ROYE Road, inclusive, and the Southern Boundary of the 1st Canadian Division.
The first bound of the 4th Canadian Division will be to the general line of the MOREUIL - DEMUIN - MARCEL CAVE Road. From here No. 1 Tank Bn., consisting of 34 Mk. V Star Tanks, each carrying two Lewis Gun and one Vickers Gun Detachments, complete with guns and ammunition, will be sent forward to assist the Cavalry in holding the BLUE DOTTED LINE.
The remainder of the Division will push forward as rapidly as possible and relieve the Cavalry in, or assist them in capturing, the BLUE DOTTED Line.

3. Location of Headquarters at ZERO.
At Zero Hour Headquarters will be located as follows :-

```
Canadian Corps    )
4th Tank Brigade  ) ................DURY.
1st Canadian Division (Adv')........T.10.d. BOIS DE
                                             GENTELLES.
2nd Canadian Division (Adv')........N.35.c.3.2.
3rd Canadian Division (Adv')........U.26.b.9.5.
4th Canadian Division (Adv')........T.1.a.6.4.
3rd Cavalry Division ...............T.3.b.2.4.
Independent Force ..................T.17.a.0.5.
```

Canadian Corps Report Centre and 4th Tank Brigade Report Centre will be established in the present Battalion H.Q. at U.7.a.6.4

4. Arrangements for Smoke Screens.
No. 2 Special Company is allotted to 3rd Canadian Division for the purpose of creating a Smoke Screen south of DODO Wood.
G.O.C.R.A. Canadian Corps will arrange to create Smoke Screens to blind the advance of the Infantry and Tanks.

(i) from observation from the high ground in C.17.central and C.18.central.

(ii) from observation from MARCEL CAVE.

(iii) from observation from WIENCOURT.

G.O.C.R.A. Canadian Corps will arrange to use smoke in the protective barrage on the GREEN LINE to conceal the Infantry and Tanks during the halt on this line.

/5.
P.T.O.

SECRET. Copy No.....

3rd Cavalry Division Order No. 41.

7th August, 1918.

Ref. Maps 1/40,000, Sheets 62E & 62D.

1. 3rd Cavalry Division, less Mobile Veterinary Sections, will move to Assembly Area 2 miles E.S.E. of LONGEAU during night 7/8th in accordance with March Table attached.
Troops will march in Sections and columns will be closed up.

2. Light Sections Cavalry Field Ambulances will accompany Brigades to his assembly areas. On arrival there they will come under orders of A.D.M.S.

3. Mobile Veterinary Sections will move from concentration area under orders of ADVS.

4. A.1 Echelons of Canadian and 7th Cavalry Brigades will follow 7th Cavalry Brigade to Starting Point and from thence 6th Cavalry Brigade.
A.1 Echelons 6th Cavalry Brigade and Divisional Troops will follow 6th Cavalry Brigade and Divisional Troops respectively to Starting Point where they will side track and from thence follow 7th Cavalry Brigade A.1 Echelon.

5. All A.2 Echelons will move to present Canadian Cavalry Brigade concentration area at R.4.d.0.0. directly Brigades and Divisional Troops have left for Starting Point and will park divisionalized under orders of Divisionalized A.2 Echelon at R.4.d.0.0. from thence as in Serial No. 7 of March Table.

6. 3rd Field Squadron will rejoin 3rd Cavalry Division in Divisional Troops Assembly Area T.2.a. & b.

7. No fires will be lighted east of AMIENS before daylight.

8. 3rd Cavalry Division Report Centre will close at PONT DE METZ at 10-0.pm. August 7th and open at Cross Tracks T.3.b.2.4. same hour.

9. Advanced Cavalry Corps Headquarters will open at Point M.29.c.7.2. (Sheet 62D) at 9-0.pm. August 7th.

10. ACKNOWLEDGE.

Lieut-Colonel,
General Staff, 3rd Cavalry Division.

Issued at 5.30 pm.

Copies to:-
1. 6th Cav.Bde.
2. 7th " "
3. Candn " "
4. 3rd Sig.Sqdn.
5. 3rd Fd.Sqdn.
6. C.R.H.A.
7. D.M.G.O.
8. "Q"
9. Aux.H.T.Coy.
10. D.A.C.
11. S.A.A.Sect.D.A.C.
12. O.C.A.S.C.
13. A.D.M.S.
14. A.D.V.S.
15. A.P.M.
16. Camp Commdt.
17. Capt. de TRAFFORD, Royals.
18. Major GOODDAY. L.S.H.
19. Cavalry Corps.
20. Canadian Corps.
21. Fourth Army.
22. 1st Cavlry Division.
23. 2nd Cavalry Division.
24. 3rd Tank Brigade.
25. Australian Corps.
26. O.C.3rd (Light)Tank Bn.
27. File. 28-30 War Diary.
31-35. Spare.

March Table issued with 3rd Cavalry Division Order No. 41.

Serial No.	Date. Aug.	Unit.	Route to Starting Pt.	Starting Point.	Time for head to pass S.P.	Route from S.P. to Assembly Area.	Assembly Area.	Remarks
1.	7th.	Canadian Cavalry Bde.	R.10.central - R.18.a.8.9.	Road junct: M.14.c.9.7.	9-45.PM.	LONGEAU - X Roads N.26.c.6.4.	Eastern side of Copse T.2.b.	
2.	7th.	7th Cavalry Brigade.	---ditto---	---do---	10-15.PM.	---ditto---	N.32.c.& d. S. of Copse at N.32.central.	
3.	7th.	6th Cavalry Brigade.	Rd.junct:R.16.a. 2.0. - X Rds R.16.d.3.0. - X Rds.M.20.a.5.9.	---do---	10-45.PM.	---ditto---	N.31.central.	
4.	7th.	Divl. H.Q. 3rd Sig.Sqn. H.Q.R.H.A.	---do---	---do---	11-15.PM.	---ditto---	Northern part of T.2.a.& b. East of GLISY-ST.NICOLAS Rd.	
5.	7th.	Divisionaliz-ed A.1 Echelon.	Canadian & 7th Cavl.Bdes as for Serial No.1. 6th & Divl.troops as for Serial No.3.	---do---	11-20.PM.	---ditto---	---ditto---	
6.	7th.	S.A.A.Sectn: D.A.C.	As for Serial No.3.	---do---	11-30.PM.	---ditto---	---ditto---	Follow Divl. Troops A.I. Echelon from S.P.
7.	8th.	Divisional-ized A.2. Echelon.	As for Serial No.1.	---do---	4-15.am.	---ditto---	---ditto---	To follow 2nd Cavy.Div: from R.tc.Central and to give preference to 2nd Cavly. Div: Fighting Trps. & A.1.Echelon & Clear S.P.at. 4-45 am.

P.T.C.

Serial No.	Date. Aug.	Unit.	Route to S.P.	Starting Point.	Time for head to pass S.P.	Route from S.P. to Assembly Area.	Assembly Area.	Remarks.
8.	8th.	Heavy Sect: D.A.C.	As for Serial No. 3.	Rd.Junction N.14.c.9.7.	4-35.AM	LONGEAU-X Rds: N.26.c.6.4.	Park at N.31.d. 2.2.	To report arrival at Assembly Area at Rear Divl.Report Centre. T.3.b.2.4
9.	8th.	Aux.H.T.Coy.	As for Serial No. 3.	--do--	4-40.AM	--do--	--do--	

"A" Form
MESSAGES AND SIGNALS.

App 7

TO: Canadian Cavalry Brigade.

Sender's Number.	Day of Month.	In reply to Number.	AAA
G.C.4.	8th		

Send leading regiment now to MORGEMONT WOOD and ascertain position of Infantry 1st and 3rd Canadian Divisions.

From: 3rd Cavalry Division.
Place: U.2.b. North of CACHY.
Time: 7.25 A.M.

(Sd) G.P.COSENS, Lt.Col.

"A" Form
MESSAGES AND SIGNALS.

Army Form C. 2121 (in pads of 100)

TO	Canadian Cav. Bde.
	3rd Light Tank Battn.

Sender's Number.	Day of Month.	In reply to Number.	AAA
G.H.1.	8		

Send remainder of your Brigade to MORGEMONT WOOD at once with 2 Coys. of Tanks.

From 3rd Cavalry Division.
Place U.2.b.
Time 7.45 A.M.

(Sd) G.P. COSENS, Lieut.-Col.

"A" Form
MESSAGES AND SIGNALS.

Army Form C. 2121

TO: 3rd Cavalry Division.

Sender's Number.	Day of Month.	In reply to Number.	AAA
B.M.5.	7th 8		

Enemy have retired IGNAUCOURT AAA Bridge intact fit for tanks AAA Two Heavy Tanks already over AAA Have started whippets to crossing IGNAUCOURT AAA Brigade moving to cross at another bridge same place.

From: Canadian Cav. Bde.
Place: N.E. MORGEMONT WOOD.
Time: 9.20 A.M.

(Sd) A.E. CONNOLLY, Major.

"A" Form
MESSAGES AND SIGNALS.

Army Form C. 2121
(in pads of 100).

TO: Cavalry Corps.

Sender's Number.	Day of Month.	In reply to Number.	
G.H.3.	8th		AAA

Canadian Cavalry Brigade have crossed river at IGNAUCOURT and are being followed by 7th Cavalry AAA Repeat Canadian Corps AAA Report Centre 3rd Cav. Div. C.13.c.5.5.

From: 3rd Cavalry Division.
Place: V.13.c.central.
Time: 10.45 A.M.

(Sd) S.G. HOWES, Major.

"A" Form
MESSAGES AND SIGNALS.

Army Form C. 2121 (in pads of 100).

TO: 3rd Cavalry Division.

Sender's Number.	Day of Month.	In reply to Number.	AAA
B.M.6.	7th 8-		

Brigade (less 2 Tanks) now over River AAA Point of assembly D.3. Infantry on RED Line strength not known AAA Will move on first objective soon as possible.

From Canadian Cav. Bde.
Place D.3. S. of IGNAUCOURT.
Time 10.20 A.M.

"A" Form
MESSAGES AND SIGNALS.

Army Form C. 2121
(in pads of 100).

TO: 3rd Cavalry Division.

Sender's Number.	Day of Month.	In reply to Number.	AAA
B.M.12	8th		

Touch obtained with M.M.Gun Brigade at MAISON BLANCHE AAA They thought they had some men in front AAA Am moving forward to straighten out situation in front of BEAUCOURT AAA Still in touch with 7th Bde. who are at same place AAA Enemy machine guns active.

From: Canadian Cav. Bde.
Place: S. of BEAUCOURT
Time: 12.50 P.M.

(Sd) A.E.CONNOLLEY, Major.

"A" Form
MESSAGES AND SIGNALS.

Army Form C. 2121
App 13

TO: 3rd Cavalry Division.

Sender's Number.	Day of Month.	In reply to Number.	AAA
G.G.3.	8th		

Brigade advancing on two Regiment front, direction North of BEAUCOURT AAA Echeloned on left flank of Canadian Cavalry Brigade AAA Intend moving with main body South of CAYEUX Wood to original objective.

From 7th Cav. Bde.
Place D.3.b.8.0.
Time 11.15 a.m.

(Z) (Sd) F.W. FITZGERALD, Capt.

"A" Form
MESSAGES AND SIGNALS.

Army Form C. 2121 (in pads of 100).

TO 3rd Cavalry Division.

Sender's Number.	Day of Month.	In reply to Number.	AAA
E.P.4.	8th		

Position is as follows 1.40 P.M. AAA Am in occupation of whole of wood S. of CAYEUX AAA Have advanced through the road through E.8.cent. and E.13.cent.. Patrols report Wood running N. and S. through E.15.central clear of enemy AAA Royals have just come up and am pushing them forward to occupy VRELY-WARVILLERS line supported by 17th Lancers and Tanks. Am moving to that position myself.

From	O.C., 7th Cav. Bde.
Place	1.45 P.M.
Time	Wood S. of CAYEUX.

(Sd) E. PATERSON, Lt.Col.

"A" Form
MESSAGES AND SIGNALS.

Army Form C. 2121 (in pads of 100)

App 15

| TO | 2nd Cav. Div. |
| | 3rd Cav. Div. |

Sender's Number.	Day of Month.	In reply to Number.	AAA
G.10	8th		

Reports received shew 1st Cav. Div. East of CAIX in E.6.c. AAA 7th Cav. Bde. reports moving on Wood in E.15.c. AAA Should the ridge in E.16.a. and c., E.22.a. and c. be occupied by the 7th Cav. Bde. you will push on through them in the direction of ROYE leaving the 3rd Cav. Div. to occupy the AMIENS outer defences as originally intended AAA The 5th Cav. Bde. will be in Corps Reserve AAA Addsd. 2nd Cav. Div. by galloper reptd. 3rd Cav. Div. Acknowledge.

From **Cavalry Corps.**
Place
Time **3.10 P.M.**

(Z) (Sd) A.F.HOME, B.G.G.S.

"A" Form.
MESSAGES AND SIGNALS.

Army Form C. 2121.
(In pads of 100.)

App 16

TO: 7th Cavalry Brigade.

Sender's Number.	Day of Month.	In reply to Number.	
G.C.13.	8th		A A A

Am ordering up 6th Cav. Bde. less Royals which are with you with orders to turn the Wood to the East of BEAUCOURT from the N. and N.E. AAA Our Infantry are in CAIX AAA I want you to push on to the dotted blue line AAAA This cancels message re concentration in D.10.c.

From: 3rd Cavalry Division
Place: D.9.b.5.5.
Time: 2.15 P.M.

(Sd) G.P.COSENS, Lt.Col.

"A" Form
MESSAGES AND SIGNALS.

Army Form C. 2121 (in pads of 100).

No. of Message: **App 7**

TO 3rd Cavalry Division.

Sender's Number.	Day of Month.	In reply to Number.	AAA
* B.M.20.	8th	G.C.16	

The state of the defences of 3rd Cav. Div. sector are approximately as follows AAA E.26.cent., E.20.d.9.0. E.21.central E.22.a.5.5. E.16.d.7.7. AAA A few forward positions are in front of the line from E.26.central to E.21.central AAA Many machine guns and Hotchkiss are employed in this Section of the line commanding the high ground E. of LE QUESNEL and BEAUFORT AAA Distribution of troops as follows AAA 7th D.G. on right flank guarding flank Inniskillings E.27.a. 17th Lancers and 10th R. Hrs. South edge of Wood E.21.a. and b. Royals from that point to E.16.d.7.7. 12th and 11th CANADIAN BDES are holding a line in conjunction with 3rd Cavalry Div. AAA Intermittent M.G. fire continues from ~~LEXQUESNEL~~ LE QUESNEL

/2

"A" Form
MESSAGES AND SIGNALS.

Army Form C. 2121
(in pads of 100).

TO -2-

Sender's Number.	Day of Month.	In reply to Number.	AAA
B.M.20			

and BEAUFORT AAA a large concentration of enemy troops at and about BEAUFORT AAA Preparations for enemy counter-attack in morning provided for as follows AAA All troops in the line in battle positions at 4 a.m. AAA 3rd Dragoon Guards intact and in hand in valley E.15. AAA Led horses of 6th Cavalry Brigade one man to four E.14.central. 7th Cavalry Bde. led horses in valley E.15. AAA C and K Batteries R.H.A. in action E.9.c. and E.14.c. respectively AAA 11th Canadian Bde. on our right and Scottish Canadian Battn. on the left AAA Ammn. O.K. AAA Water carts badly wanted AAA By request of Col. PATERSON I have taken over command of the divisional sector for the night.

From 6th Cavalry Bde.
Place E.14.d.8.8.
Time 11.25 P.M.

(Sd) F.H.W.C. WHITMORE,
Lt. Col.

6th Cavalry Brigade.	3rd Fd.Sqdn.	"Q"	Cav. Corps.
7th Cavalry Brigade.	A.D.M.S.	1st Cav. Div.	
Can. Cavalry Brigade.	A.D.V.S.	2nd Cav. Div.	

G.C.22.   10th.

Cavalry Corps will have one Divn. ready to advance with 2 Divisions in reserve.AAA 3rd Cavalry Division will be ready to advance AAA in consequence 6th Cavalry Brigade will send patrols to take over from 2nd Cavalry Division on the front BOUCHOIR ROUVROY (both inclusive) and the 7th Cavalry Brigade to take over from 1st Cavalry Division on the front ROUVROY exclusive, MEHARICOURT, ROSIERES,inclusive AAA Dividing line between Brigades VRELY, FOUQUESCOURT, HATTENCOURT, all inclusive to 6th Cavalry Brigade.AAA Patrols will move out at 5 a.m. 10th AAA Main body will move 5.30 a.m. to position of readiness in E.15.a. & b. with Divisional H.Q. at E.16.d.9.5. AAA Order of march 6th, 7th and Canadian Cavalry Brigades, 3rd Field Squadron AAA1st and 2nd Cavalry Divisions will complete their withdrawal to an area about CAIX and CAYEUX as soon as patrols of 7thaand 6th Cavalry Brigades are in position on their front AAA 3rd Tank Bde. will send as many tanks as are available to co-operate with 3rd Cavalry Division in event of an advance. Divl. Report Centre moves to E.16.d.9.5. at 5.30 a.m. AAA Acknowledge AAA Addressed 3 Bdes., 3rd Fd.Sqdn., Q, A.D.M.S. A.D.V.S. reptd 1st and 2nd Cav. Divs and Cavalry Corps.

3rd Cavalry Division.
E.1.d.8.2.
2.45 a.m.   (Sd) G.P.COSENS, Lt.Col.

"A" Form.
MESSAGES AND SIGNALS.

Army Form C. 2121.
(In pads of 100.)

TO	6th Cavalry Brigade.

Sender's Number.	Day of Month.	In reply to Number.	
G.C.23.	10th	B.M.47	AAA

H.Q. 2nd Cav. Div. at E.30.a.3.7. (1,000 N.E. of WARVILLERS) AAA Strength of patrols not known AAA It is probable most of Cavalry have been relieved by Infantry but there will be some advanced patrols still out on line mentioned AAA Your patrols should get in touch with 2nd C.B.H.Q.

From 3rd Cav. Div.

(Sd) G.P. COSENS, Lt.Col.

MESSAGES AND SIGNALS.

Army Form C. 2121
(In pads of 100.)

TO: 7th Cavalry Brigade.

Sender's Number	Day of Month	In reply to Number	AAA
G.C.24	10th		

In continuation of G.C.22 AAA H.Q. 1st Cav. Div. at F.13.d.2.5. VRELY AAA Your patrols should get in touch with 1st Cav. Div. H.Q. and find out what patrols they have still out.

From: 3rd Cavalry Division.

(Sd) G.P.COSENS, Lt.Col.

app 21

```
6th Cav. Bde.      3rd Fd.Sqdn.     A.D.V.S.         Cav. Corps.
7th Cav. Bde.      3rd Sig.Sqdn.    1st Cav.Div.
Can.Cav.Bde.       A.D.M.S.         2nd Cav. Div.
```

G.C.25.   10th.

1.   Canadian Corps has reached line BOUCHOIR - WARVILLERS - VRELY - ROSIERES. Advanced infantry and tanks operating with Cavalry near ROUVROY-MEHARICOURT Road. French are fighting in ARVILLERS on our right. Australians on our left have reached VAUVILLERS and FRAMERVILLE in touch with us on railway in F.5.

2.   Canadian Corps will continue advance today to general line ROYE - HATTENCOURT - HALLU - French will advance on HILL 88 - ANDECHY - VILLERS LES ROYE on our immediate right. Left French Division is 126th Divn. Australian Corps on our left will advance on LIHONS.

3.   32nd Division on right and 4th Canadian Division on left will advance at 8 a.m. to the line mentioned in para. 2.
   Corps Boundaries.
   Northern   ... AMIENS - NESLE Road.
   Southern   ... ROYE Rd. inclusive - LA CAMBUSE X roads thence
                  via GUYENCOURT (exclusive) to GRUNY (inclusive).

   Inter-Divisional Boundaries.

   ROUVROY - FOUQUESCOURT - FRANSART - HATTENCOURT (all inclusive) to 4th Canadian Divn.

4.   1, 2, 3 Canadian Divisions will be in Corps Reserve and remain on the line gained yesterday consolidating it as a main line of defence to be held in event of counter-attack driving in our leading Divisions.

5.   Artillery. In addition to their own artillery, 1 Divisional Artillery and one Brigade R.G.A. will be allotted to 32nd Division, and 2 A.F.A. Brigades and 1 Brigade R.G.A. to 4th Canadian Division. 1 Tank Battn. is allotted to 4th Canadian Division.

6.   Headquarters. At commencement Report Centres of Divisions will be as follows:-
   32nd Div. H.Q. at Adv. H.Q. 3rd Canadian Div. D.28.a.9.9.
   Adv. 1st Canadian V.23.d.7.5.
   Brigades will work on a broad front with patrols and Squadrons in close touch with infantry advance and co-operating closely with it.
   The Canadian Cav. Bde. will be in support at about E.16.cent.

8.   Medical.
   M.D.S. at T.17.d.central.
   C.F.A. in Chateau at V.27.b.5.0.at IGNAUCOURT.
   C.F.A. now moving along CAYEUX-CAIX Rd. will open S. of CAIX and patrol roads to VRELY & MEHARICOURT.
   C.F.A. moving through LE QUESNEL patrolling roads BEAUFORT and WARVILLERS.

9.   Veterinary. Adv. M.V.S. at CAIX.

10. Report Centre E.16.d.6.5. As situation develops it will be moved to E.30.a. cross tracks near Windmill.

3rd Cavalry Division.   (Sd) G.P.COSENS, Lt.Col.

"A" Form
MESSAGES AND SIGNALS.

Army Form C. 2121
(In pads of 100.)

TO	3rd Cavalry Division.

Sender's Number.	Day of Month	In reply to Number.	AAA
B.M.154	10th		

G.O.C. 32nd Div. interviewed here 11.30 a.m. says LA CHAVETTE, PARVILLERS, are taken and probably DAMERY AAA Brigade H.Q. moving to clump of trees half way between FOLIE and WARVILLERS AAA No news from advanced regts. yet AAA G.O.C. 32nd Div. reports enemy quite demoralised P.B. men employed on defence and being hunted along from pillar to post.

From: 6th Cavalry Brigade.
Place: 800 x N. of FOLIES Church.
Time: 11.45 a.m.

(Sd) D.E. WALLACE, Capt.

"A" Form
MESSAGES AND SIGNALS.

Army Form C. 2121
(In pads of 100.)
No. of Message........ 23

Prefix....Code....m.	Words	Charge.	This message is on a/c of:	Recd. at....m.
Office of Origin and Service Instructions	Sent At ....m.		....Service....	Date
	To			From
	By		(Signature of "Franking Officer")	By

TO — Cavalry Corps.

Sender's Number.	Day of Month.	In reply to Number.	AAA
G.S.46	10th		

G.O.C. 32nd Divn. says LA CHAVETTE - PARVILLERS taken and probably DAMERY AAA 6th Cav. Bde. H.Q. moving to clump of trees halfway between FOLIE and WARVILLERS AAA No news advanced regiments yet AAA G.O.C. 32nd Div. reports enemy quite demoralised P.B. men employed in defence and being hunted along from pillar to post.

From: 3rd Cavalry Divn.
Place:
Time:

The above may be forwarded as now corrected. (Z) (Sd.) C. SWIRE, Capt. G.S.

"A" Form
MESSAGES AND SIGNALS.

Army Form C. 2121
(In pads of 100.)

TO 6th Cavalry Brigade.

Sender's Number.	Day of Month.	In reply to Number.	AAA
G.C.29.	10th	B.M.54.	

Reference your report push on at once to objective with all possible speed AAA Divisional Report Centre moving to E.30a.a AAA 16 tanks (Whippets) being sent to join you at FOLIES AAA Leave a guide there to bring them on.

From G.O.C. 3rd Cav. Div.

(Sd.) G.P.COSENS, Lt.Col.

"A" Form
MESSAGES AND SIGNALS.

Army Form C. 2121
(In pads of 100.)

TO: 3rd Cavalry Division

Sender's Number.	Day of Month.	In reply to Number.	AAA
B.M.55	10th		

G.O.C., 97th Inf. Bde. confirms capture of LA CHAVETTE AAA Leading Squadron 3rd D.Gs. went to LE QUESNOY at 11.50 a.m. AAA Main body Royals now W. edge of ROUVROY AAA

From 6th Cavalry Brigade.
Place 1000 x N.E. FOLIE Ch.
Time 12.15 P.M.

(Sd) D.E. WALLACE, Capt.

"A" Form.
MESSAGES AND SIGNALS.

Army Form C.2121.

TO { 6th Cav. Bde.
     7th Cav. Bde.

Sender's Number.	Day of Month.	In reply to Number.	A A A
G.H.32	10th		

As the situation develops and the Infantry advance, G.O.C. wants reports as to suitability of ground up to and beyond our objective for the employment of Cavalry mounted moving fast in large numbers AAA Would suggest special Officers patrol to be detailed for this purpose.

From 3rd Cavalry Division.

Time 11.5 a.m.

(Sd) S.G. HOWES, Major

Service Instructions	Words	Charge	This message is on a/c of:	Recd. at ......m.
	Sent			Date
	At ......m.		Service	From
	To			
	By		(Signature of "Franking Officer")	By

TO — Cavalry Corps.

Sender's Number.	Day of Month	In reply to Number	AAA
G.C.31	10th		

7th Cav. Bde. reports all ground E. of line MEHARICOURT - ROUVROY EN SANTERRE up to the objective between CHAULNES ROSIERES Rly. and the line FRANSART ROUVROY impassable for Cavalry except in small numbers AAA Therefore I have brought 7th Cav. Bde. into reserve just W. of ROUVROY EN SANTERRE and am sending on Canadian Cav. Bde. supported by 6th Cav. Bde. to seize high ground N. and E. of ROYE.

From 3rd Cavalry Division.
Place E.30.a.
Time 2.15 P.M.

(Sd) G.P.COSENS, Lt.Col.

"A" Form.
MESSAGES AND SIGNALS.

TO: 6th Cav. Bde.
7th Cava. Bde.

Sender's Number.	Day of Month.	In reply to Number.	AAA
G.H.32	10th		

As the situation develops and the Infantry advance, G.O.C. wants reports as to suitability of ground up to and beyond our objective for the employment of Cavalry mounted moving fast in large numbers AAA Would suggest Special Officers patrol to be detailed for this purpose.

From 3rd Cavalry Div.
Place
Time 11.5 a.m.

(Sd.) S.G. HOWES, Major.

TO: 3rd Cavalry Division

Sender's Number.	Day of Month.	In reply to Number.	AAA
BM.60	10th	G.H.32.	

2 Officers patrols were sent out from here to report on the ground on the Brigade front especially towards PARVILLERS AAA They report that there is an old trench system about the line ROUVROY - LE QUESNOY and that the movement of large bodies of Cavalry at any pace would be quite impossible AAA Both advanced regiments have made similar reports and state that any further advance on present front must be made dismounted.

From: 6th Cavalry Brigade.
Place: 100 N.E. of FOLIE Ch.
Time: 2.35 P.M.

(Sd) F.H.D.C.WHITMORE, Lt.Col.

MESSAGES AND SIGNALS.

TO: 6th Cavalry Brigade.
Canadian Cav. Bde.

Sender's Number.	Day of Month.	In reply to Number.	AAA
G.C.32	10th		

Canadian Cavalry Bde. less 1 Regiment have orders to go through and seixe high ground N. and E. of ROYE AAA You should support them AAA Am bringing 7th Cav. Bde. into Reserve S.W. of ROUVROY where I am moving my report centre AAA

Addsd 6th Cav. Bde. reptd. Canadian Cav. Bde.

From Place: 3rd Cav. Div.

(Sd) G.P.COSENS, Lt.Col.

"A" Form.
MESSAGES AND SIGNALS.

Army Form C. 2121.
(In pads of 100.)

TO	1st Cav. Div.	Fourth Army.
	2nd Cav. Div.	Canadian Corps
	3rd Cav. Div.	Aust. Corps.

Sender's Number.	Day of Month.	In reply to Number.	AAA
G.51.	10th		

Reports shew that the enemy's resistance is weakening all along the line AAA 3rd Cav. Div. will push on and occupy the high ground N. of ROYE AAA 2nd Cav. Div. will push forward and occupy NESLE AAA Addsd 2nd & 3rd Cav. Divs. reptd 1st Cav. Div. Fourth Army, Australian and Canadian Corps.

From Cavalry Corps.

Time 2.25 P.M.

(Sd) A. E. HOME. B.G.

"A" Form.
MESSAGES AND SIGNALS.

| TO | 7th Cavalry Brigade. |

Sender's Number.	Day of Month.	In reply to Number.	
G.C.33	10th		A A A

As ground in front of you reported impassable concentrate your Brigade just W. of ROUVROY EN SANTERRE AAA Am moving my report centre to S.W. corner of ROUVROY.

From 3rd Cav. Div.
Place E.30.a.
Time 2.10 P.M.

(Sd.) G.P. COSENS. Lt. Col

"A" Form.
MESSAGES AND SIGNALS.

Army Form C. 2121.
(In pads of 100.)

No. of Message..................

| Prefix......Code............m | Words. | Charge. | This message is on a/c of: | Recd. at............m. |
| Office of........and Service Instructions. | Sent At............m. To...... By...... | | Service (Signature of "Franking Officer.") | Date From By...... |

Cpp 33

TO Cavalry Corps.

Sender's Number.	Day of Month.	In reply to Number.	
G.C.35	10th		A A A

Ordered Canadian Cav. Bde. to seize high ground North and East of ROYE and to proceed South of the AMIENS-ROYE Road as the ground to the North of it is quite impassable for Cavalry but I do not consider that it will be possible for them to carry out their mission as the line runs through or West of ANDECHY - LA CAMBUSE - W. of DAMERY and W. of PARVILLERS AAA Canadian Brigade moved forward at about 3.45 P.M. but so far I have not had any information AAA

From 3rd Cavalry Division.
Place
Time 4.47 P.M.

(Z) (Sd) G.P.COSENS, Lt.Col.

MESSAGES AND SIGNALS.

TO: 6th Cavalry Brigade.

Sender's Number.	Day of Month.	In reply to Number.	A A A
G.C.38	10th		

Canadian Cav. Brigade have galloped HILL 100 with one Regt. and are now there AAA You must support them closely and keep in close touch with them.

From Place: G.O.C. 3rd Cav. Div.

(Sd) G.P.COSENS, Lt.Col.

"A" Form
MESSAGES AND SIGNALS.

Army Form C. 2121
(In pads of 100.)

Prefix....Code....m	Words	Charge	This message is on a/c of:	Recd. at....m
Office of Origin and Service Instructions	Sent At....m			Date
	To			From
	By		(Signature of "Franking Officer")	By

TO 3rd Cavalry Division.

Sender's Number.	Day of Month	In reply to Number	AAA
B.M.29	10th		

Our infantry now attacking Wood in R.3.b. AAA
F.G.H. galloping point 100 are now there AAA
Will move forward if possible AAA Some dismtd.
Cavalry on left of road (in trench) about
R.2.b.

From Canadian Cav. Bde.
Place
Time 5.5. p.m.

The above may be forwarded as now corrected.   (Z)   (Sd) C.E.CONNOLEY, Major

"A" Form
MESSAGES AND SIGNALS.

Army Form C. 2121 (In pads of 100.)

TO: 3rd Cavalry Division

Sender's Number.	Day of Month.	In reply to Number.	AAA
B.M.30	10th		

Enemy still holding DAMERY and PARVILLERS AAA Attempted to take point 100 by charge along ROYE ROAD but 3 troops wiped out AAA Enemy holding wood strongly with M.Gs. and also small wood N. of LA CAMBUSE AAA French now hold ANDECHY and ARVILLERS LE ROYE AAA I have one Squadron in VILLERS LE ROYE (F.G.H.) held up by M.G. fire from wood S. of GOYENCOURT AAA Our infantry line now runs R.3.cent. - L.33.d. cent. - just W. of PARVILLERS - L.28.a. AAA French state they advanced without opposition from GUERBIGNY to L'ECHELLE along river valley AAA Our infantry are not advancing AAA Country off the road impossible for horses owing to wire and trenches.

From: Canadian Cav. Bde.
Place: R.2.b.cent.
Time: 5.30 P.M.

(Sd) C.E.CONNOLEY, Major.

"A" Form.
MESSAGES AND SIGNALS.

TO	3rd Cavalry Division

Sender's Number.	Day of Month.	In reply to Number.	AAA
B.M.66	10th	G.C.38	

10th Hussars being sent to support F.G.H. AAA
Royals moving to N. edge of FOLIES AAA
Brigade report centre to windmill N. of B. of
BOUCHOIR

From: 6th Cavalry Bde.
Place:
Time: 5.50 P.M.

Censor: D.F. WALLACE

"A" Form.
MESSAGES AND SIGNALS.

Army Form C. 2121.
(In pads of 100.)

app 39

TO: Capt. JENKINS, O.C. Div. B. Echelon.
O.C. Heavy Sect. Reserve Park.

Sender's Number.	Day of Month.	In reply to Number.	
G.75/1	12th		A A A

Reference 1/100,000 AMIENS.

3rd Cav. Div. "B" Echelon and Heavy Sections C.F.A. and Heavy Sect. 3rd Cav. Reserve Park will move forthwith to rejoin 3rd Cav. Div. in area BOIS DE BOVES to COTTENCHY - GUYENCOURT - JUMEL - REMIENCOURT - DOMMARTIN FOUENCAMPS AAA

Route CAVILLON - BRIQUEMESNIL - FLUY - CREUSE - PLACHY ST. SAUFLIEU, thence to Brigade and Divisional Troops areas.

"B" Echelons will rejoin their Brigades on arrival in Divisional area. Heavy Sects. C.F.As will rejoin Light Sects. C.F.As areas.

Divl. H.Q. at FM. 1 mile S.S.W. of B of B.de BOVES.

6th Cav. Bde. FOUENCAMPS & DOMMARTIN.
7th Cav. Bde. GUYENCOURT & JUMEL.
Can. Cav. Bde. COTTENCHY & LE PARACLET.

/2

"A" Form.
MESSAGES AND SIGNALS.

Army Form C. 2121.

Sender's Number.	Day of Month.	In reply to Number.	
G.75/1	12th		A A A

TO -2-

Divisional Troops area REMIENCOURT.

Fourth Army traffic distances will be maintained, i.e. 25 yds. between groups of every 6 vehicles.

Addsd Capt. JENKINS, 7th D.Gs., O.C. Heavy Sect. 3rd Cav. Res. Pk. repeated 3 Bdes, Field Sqdn, C.R.H.A., "Q", A.D.M.S., A.D.VS, A.P.M., Camp Commdt., O.C. A.S.C. Fourth Army and Cav. Corps

From 3rd Cavalry Division.
Place B. of BOIS de BOVES.
Time 3.30 P.M.

(Sd) S.G. HOWES, Major,

App. 40

SECRET.

Copy No. 22

3rd Cavalry Division Order No. 42.

Reference 1/100,000 Sheet 17 AMIENS.   15th August, 1918.

1. In continuation of G.X.200/26 dated 15th August, the Division will march during the night 15th/16th August in accordance with March Table overleaf. Troops to be in Camp by 4.30 a.m. 16th.

2. "A" and "B" Echelons will accompany Brigades.

3. Distances laid down in Fourth Army Orders to be maintained from Starting Point.

4. Divisional Report Centre will close at SAINS EN AMIENOIS at 7 P.M. and re-open at YZEUX Chateau at the same hour.

5. Railhead 16th AMIENS (Main Station), 17th HANGEST.

6. ACKNOWLEDGE.

Lieut.Colonel,
G.S., 3rd Cavalry Division.

Issued at 1 P.M.

Copy No.
1 to 6th Cav. Brigade.
2 " 7th "
3 " Canadian Cav. Bde.
4 " 3rd Signal Sqdn.
5 " 3rd Field Squadron.
6 " C.R.H.A.
7 " D.M.G.O.
8 " "Q"
9 " D.A.C.
10 " 3rd Cav. Reserve Park.
11 " Aux. H.T. Company.
12 " A.D.M.S.
13 " A.D.V.S.
14 " A.P.M.
15 " O.C. A.S.C.
16 " Camp Commandant.

March Table issued with 3rd Cavalry Division Order No. 42.

1	2	3	4	5	6	7	8
Serial No.	Date.	Unit.	Starting Point.	Time to pass S.P.	Route.	Destination	Remarks.
1	August 15th	7th Cavalry Bde.	BOVES Church	8.30 P.M.	BOUTILLERIE - ST. of ST.ACHEUL - AMIENS Main Station - thence N.of River to LONGPRE - ST.SAUVEUR - ST.VAST	ST. OUEN.	Tail of 7th Cav. Bde. to be clear of COTTENCHY by 8.45 P.M.
2	do.	Canadian Cav. Brigade.	X Roads & tracks 1100 yds. S. of 1st C in COTTENCHY	9.30 P.M.	ST.FUSCIEN - Road junction N. of E in AMIENS - Southern & Western outskirts of AMIENS - MONTIERES - PICQUIGNY - HANGEST.	HANGEST BOURDON.	Cndn.Cav.Bde. when moving to S.P. to keep way clear for 7th Cav.Brigade.
3	do.	6th Cav.Brigade.	E. exit of ESTREES SUR NOYE.	9.45 P.M.	RUMIGNY - VERS - CLAIRY SAULCHOIX - PISSY - FLUY - BRIQUE MESNIL - CAVILLON.	SOUES - LA REGE - FIENCOURT	Tail to be clear of DOMMARTIN Church by 9.45 P.M. to march to S.P. via DOMMARTIN Ch. thence road junction at S. exit COTTEN-CHY but not to enter COTTENCHY
4	do.	Field Sqdn. Reserve Park. D.A.C. Aux.H.T.Coy.	D of DOMMARTIN	9.45 P.M.	FOUENCAMPS - BOVES Church - thence as for Serial No.1 to ST. VAST EN CHAUSSEE, thence via VIGNACOURT.	BETHENCOURT ST. OUEN.	In order of march as shown in Column 3.
5	do.	Divl. H.Q. H.Q. R.H.A. 3rd Sig.Sqdn. H.Q. A.S.C.	N. exit of SAINS EN AMIENOIS	9 P.M.	ST.FUSCIEN - Road junct. N. of E. in AMIENS - Southern & Western outskirts of AMIENS - PICQUIGNY - MONTIERES - PICQUIGNY - LA CHAUSSEE - BELLOY.	YZEUX.	

"A" Form.
MESSAGES AND SIGNALS.

Army Form C. 2121.

App. 41

TO All concerned.

Sender's Number.	Day of Month.	In reply to Number.	AAA
G.130	20th		

Brigades and units of Divisional Troops will be ready to move at 3 hours notice from receipt of orders at Brigade and Unit H.Q. AAA Acknowledge AAA Addsd all concerned.

From 3rd Cavalry Division.

G.P. COSENS, Lt.Col.

App. 42

SECRET.

Copy No....19....

3rd Cavalry Division Order No. 44.

August 21st, 1918.

Reference 1/100,000 Sheets 11 and 17, LENS & AMIENS.

1. 6th Cavalry Brigade and Canadian Cavalry Brigade will move tonight in accordance with March Table overleaf.
   6th Cavalry Brigade H.Q. to be at FIEFFES and Canadian Cavalry Brigade H.Q. at DOMART EN PONTHIEU.

2. "A" Echelons and Light Sections C.F.As. will accompany Brigades.
   "B" Echelons and Heavy Sections C.F.As. will march to BETHENCOURT ST. OUEN as stated overleaf in Serial Nos. 2 and 4.

3. Distances to be maintained as laid down in S.S. 724, para. 19, page 2.

4. No movement before 8 P.M. and Brigades will not enter their new areas before 10 P.M.

5. The remainder of the Division will not move.

6. Divisional H.Q. will remain at YZEUX.

7. ACKNOWLEDGE.

Issued at 7.50 P.M.

Lieut.Colonel,
G.S., 3rd Cavalry Division.

Copies to:-
No. 1. 6th Cavalry Brigade.
    2. 7th Cavalry Brigade.
    3. Canadian Cavalry Brigade.
    4. 3rd Field Squadron R.E.
    5. 3rd Signal Squadron.
    6. C.R.H.A.
    7. "Q".
    8. A.D.M.S.
    9. A.D.V.S.
   10. A.P.M.
   11. O.C. A.S.C.
   12. Third Army.
   13. Fourth Army.
   14. Cavalry Corps.
   15. Aux. H.T. Company.
   16. File.
17-19. War Diary.
   20.
   21.

March Table issued with 3rd Cavalry Division Order No. 44.

Serial No.	Date.	Unit.	Starting Point.	Time to Pass S.P.	Route.	Destination.	Remarks.
1.	Night Aug.21/22	6th Cavalry Bde. less "B" Echelon & Heavy Section C.F.A.			PICQUIGNY - LA CHAUSSEE - VIGNACOURT - CANAPLES.	FIEFFES - MONTRELET - BONNEVILLE area.	(i) Bde. H.Q. will be established at FIEFFES. (ii) Billets from Area Commdt., FIEFFES.
2.	do.	"B" Echelon & Heavy Section C.F.A. of 6th Cavalry Bde.			HANGEST L. FLIXECOURT.	BETHENCOURT ST. OUEN.	(i) Not to enter HANGEST before 12 midnight. (ii) To report to O.C.,A.H.T.Coy. at BETHENCOURT ST.OUEN for billets and bivouac area.
3.	do.	Canadian Cav.Bde. less "B" Echelon & Heavy Section C.F.A.			FLIXECOURT (S.E. exit) - ST. LEGER LES DOMART.	DOMART-EN-PONTHIEU - ST. HILAIRE.	(i) Bde. H.Q.will be established at DOMART EN PONTHIEU. (ii) Canadian Cav. Bde. & "B" Echelon & Heavy Sect.C.F.A. to be clear of BOURDON by 12 midnight. (iii) Billets from Area Commandant, DOMART EN PONTHIEU.
4.	do.	"B" Echelon & Heavy Section C.F.A. of Canadian Cav.Bde.			BOURDON - FLIXECOURT.	BETHENCOURT ST. OUEN.	(i) To follow Canadian Cav. Bde. to BETHENCOURT ST.OUEN & break off there. (ii) To report to O.C.,A.H.T.Coy. at BETHENCOURT ST.OUEN for billets and bivouac area.

War Diary   App 43

SECRET.

3rd Cavalry Division Order No.45.   Copy No...... 22

25th August, 1918.

Reference 1/100,000 Sheets 11, 14, 17, LENS, ABBEVILLE, AMIENS.

1.   3rd Cavalry Division will move tonight, 25/26th August to an area West of AUXI LE CHATEAU in accordance with March Table attached. Brigade Headquarters will be as Column 6 of attached Table.

2.   "A" Echelons and Light Sections C.F.As. will accompany Brigades.

3.   "B" Echelons and Heavy Sections C.F.As. of 6th and Canadian Cavalry Brigades will march as per Table under Officers detailed to command Brigade "B" Echelons, and will rejoin Brigades at end of march.
       "B" Echelon and Heavy Section C.F.A., 7th Cavalry Brigade, will accompany Brigade.

4.   Distances to be maintained as laid down in S.S.724, para.19, page 2.

5.   March will take place between the hours of 8 p.m. and 5 a.m. and all units will be in bivouac by 5 A.M.

6.   Divisional Headquarters will close at YZEUX Chateau, 9.30 P.M. August 25th and re-open at FONTAINE L'ETALON at the same hour.

7.   Acknowledge.

Issued at..6.0..P.M.   G.S., 3rd Cavalry Division.   Lieut.Colonel,

Copy No. 1.   6th Cavalry Brigade.
         2.   7th Cavalry Brigade.
         3.   Canadian Cavalry Brigade.
         4.   3rd Field Squadron R.E.
         5.   3rd Signal Squadron.
         6.   C.R.H.A.
         7.   "Q".
         8.   A.D.M.S.
         9.   A.D.V.S.
     10.   A.P.M.
     11   Camp Commandant.
   12-13   O.C. A.S.C.
     14   Aux. H.T.Company.
     15   O.C. "B" Echelon 6th Cav. Bde.
     16.   do.   do.   Canadian Cav. Bde.
     17.   Third Army.
     18   Fourth Army.
     19   Cavalry Corps.
     20   1. D.A.C.
     21   .   3rd Cav.Res.Park.

March Table issued with 3rd Cavalry Division Order No. 45.

Serial No.	Date.	Unit.	Starting Point.	Time to pass S.P.	Route.	Destination.	Remarks
1.	Night Aug. 25/26	6th Cavalry Bde.	S. exit of FIENVILLERS	10 P.M.	FIENVILLERS - BERNAVILLE - PROUVILLE - MAIZICOURT - AUXI-LE-CHATEAU.	Area:- GUESCHART - WILLENCOURT - LE PONCHEL - VITZ - VILLEROY - VILLEROYE S/Authie - CUMONVILLE.	Brigade H.Q. GUESCHART.
2.	do.	Canadian Cavalry Brigade.	S. exit of RIBEAUCOURT.	9 P.M.	RIBEAUCOURT - BEAUMETZ - AGENVILLE - MAISON PONTHIEU - GUESCHART.	Area:- BOUFFLERS - TOLLENT - LABROYE - GENNE IVERGNY.	(i) Bde.H.Q. BOUFFLERS. (ii) Accommodation in GENNE IVERGNY is partly occupied by 2nd Cav. Div. "B" Echelon.
3.	do.	7th Cav. Bde. with B Echelon & Heavy Section C.F.A.	2nd S of SURCAMPS.	9 P.M.	CHAUSEE BRUNEHAUT via YVRENCH and NOYELLES, thence by main ABBEVILLE HESDIN Road to LE BOISLE.	Area:- TORTEFONTAINE - RAYE SUR AUTHIE - LE BOISLE - RAPECHY VOISIN - LEMOULINEL - FONDEVAL.	Bde. H.Q. LE BOISLE.
4.	do.	Field Squadron. D.A.C. Aux.H.T.Coy. Reserve Park. (Light & Heavy Sections).	N.W.exit of ST. OUEN.	10 P.M.	Follow Serial No.3 to LE BOISLE thence via TOLLENT.	GAUMONT. CAUMONT. CAUMONT. CAUMONT.	(i) In order of march as in Column 3. (ii) To report to C.R.H.A. at CAUMONT for accommodation.

P.T.O.

-2-

Serial No.	Date.	Unit.	Starting Point.	Time to pass S.P.	Route.	Destination.	Remarks.
5.	Night Aug. 25/26.	Div. H.Q. H.Q. R.H.A. " A.S.C. 3rd Sig.Sqdn.	Road junction 800 yards. N. of B of BOIS DE GARD.	9.30 P.M.	2nd O of BETHENCOURT ST. OUEN.- S.E. exit of ST. OUEN - ST. LEGER LES DOMART - DOMART - RIBEAUCOURT - BEAUMETZ - PROUVILLE Church - MAIZICOURT - AUXI LE CHATEAU - LE PONCHEL - VE of GENNE-IVERGNY.	FONTAINE L'ETALON 1. FONTAINE L'ETALON in Column 3. FONTAINE L'ETALON	In order of march as CAUMONT. 2.C.R.H.A. to allot accommodation in CAUMONT.
6.	do.	"B" Echelon & Heavy Section of Canadian Cav. Bde. "B" Echelon & Heavy Section C.F.A. of 6th Cavalry Bde.	Follow Reserve Park in Serial No. 4.	--	Route as for Serial No.4. to NOYELLES EN CHAUSSEE, thence via GUESCHART.	Canadian Cavalry Bde. area. 6th Cavalry Brigade area.	To rejoin Bdes in their areas. do.

War Diary   App 44

SECRET.

Copy No......

3rd Cavalry Division Order No. 46.

26th August, 1918.

Reference Map 1/100,000, LENS 11.

1. 3rd Cavalry Division will move forthwith as follows:-

    6th Cavalry Brigade. ... To NUNCQ - SIBIVILLE - SERICOURT - PIT BOURET - GRAND BOURET.

    Route: AUXI LE CHATEAU - FREVENT.

    Canadian Cavalry Bde. ... To MONCHEL - HAUTE COTE - LIGNY SUR CANCHE - PETIT BOUBERS.

    Route: LE PONCHEL - VAULX - BUIRE AU BOIS - MONCHEL.

    7th Cavalry Brigade. ... To CONCHY - AUBROMETZ - FILLIEVRES.

    Route: CAUMONT - QUOEUX.

    Divisional Troops.

3rd Field Squadron, R.E.	To GALAMETZ.		) Will
4th Bde. R.H.A.) D.A.C.)	" WILLEMAN.	Route - Any.	) not move) until) 7th Cav.) Bde. have
Light Section, Reserve Park.	" WAIL.	Route - Any.	) passed) through) their area

"B" Echelons, Heavy Sections C.F.As., Heavy Section Reserve Park and Aux. H.T. Company will move to WILLENCOURT when Brigades are clear of their areas and will be divisionalized under Captain PRATT, 6th Dragoons.

    Divisional H.Q. and 3rd Signal Squadron ... To WAIL. Route Any

2. Divisional Headquarters will close at FONTAINE L'ETALON at 5 P.M. and re-open at WAIL at the same hour.

3. Acknowledge.

C Swire Capt
for
Lieut. Colonel,
G.S., 3rd Cavalry Division.

Issued at 3.45 P.M.
26.8.18.

Copy No. 1 to 6th Cav. Bde.   11 to Camp Commandant.
         2 " 7th Cav. Bde.   12-13" O.C. A.S.C.
         3 " Can. Cav. Bde.   14 " Aux. H.T. Company.
         4 " 3rd Fd. Sqdn. R.E.   15 " D.A.C.
         5 " 3rd Signal Sqdn.   16 " 3rd Cav. Res. Park.
         6 " C.R.H.A.   17 " Third Army.
         7 " "Q".   18 " Cavalry Corps.
         8 " A.D.M.S.
         9 " A.D.V.S.
        10 " A.P.M.

"A" Form.
MESSAGES AND SIGNALS.
Army Form C. 2121.

TO: All concerned.

Sender's Number.	Day of Month.	In reply to Number.	
G.209	31st		A A A

Brigades and units of Divisional troops will be prepared to move in 6 hours from receipt of orders at their H.Q. AAA Addsd all concerned.

From 3rd Cav. Div.
Time 9.45 a.m.

(Sd) S.G. HOWES, Major, G.S.

Confidential

War Diary
of
General Staff
3rd Cavalry Division
Intelligence Summaries
September, 1918

GENERAL STAFF
7/10/18
3rd CAVALRY DIVISION

(6339) Wt. W150/M3016 1,500,000 10/17 McA & W Ltd (E1898) Forms W3091.   Army Form W.3091.

Cover for Documents.

Nature of Enclosures.

Notes, or Letters written.

Appendix 1

REPORT ON THE OPERATIONS EAST OF ARRAS IN WHICH THE

10th (P.W.O.) ROYAL HUSSARS TOOK PART ON SEPT. 2nd, 1918.

1. Friday, August 30th. The 10th Royal Hussars received orders to march to WAILLY to take part in the operations of the Canadian Corps, organized for the purpose of breaking through the DROCOURT-QUEANT Line astride the CAMBRAI Road, and thence swinging outwards rolling up the line to North and South.

2. Sunday, September 1st. At a conference held at the Citadel, ARRAS, Lt.Col. F.H.D.C.WHITMORE, C.M.G., D.S.O., commanding 10th Royal Hussars, received orders to command the Leading Group of the Independent Force.
    This Independent Force, commanded by Brig.Gen. R.BRUTINEL, C.M.G., D.S.O., consisted of the following troops:-

    10th Royal Hussars.
    Canadian Light Horse.
    1st and 2nd Canadian M.M.G.Brigade.
    Canadian Cyclist Battalion.
    1 Battery C.F. Artillery.
    2 Sections Medium Trench Mortars.
    6 Heavy Armoured Cars (17th Tank Battalion).
    2 Light Armoured Cars (2nd Canadian M.M.G.Brigade).
    1 Wireless Section.
    1 Supply Column.

    The role of this Force was as follows:-
    As soon as the RED Line was captured by the 1st Canadian, 4th Canadian and 4th British Divisions, the Force was to advance through the RED Line and seize the Canal crossing at MARQUION and form a bridge head on the high ground East of that place.
    The protective barrage proceeding onwards from the RED Line at ZERO + 120 minutes, i.e. 8.0 a.m., being tabled to be clear of MARQUION at ZERO + 6½ hours having advanced at the rate of 2000 yds. per hour. At the same time a rectangular area 1000 yards astride the main CAMBRAI Road was provided, along which the barrage moved at the rate of 1000 yards per 10 minutes, thus allowing the Independent Force to proceed at the rate of 6000 yards in one hour in this rectangular area.
    The rectangular area included 500 yards on either side of the main road as shewn in Canadian Corps Barrage Map "A".

3.(a) The Leading Group under Lt.Col. WHITMORE, C.M.G., D.S.O., consisted of the following troops:-

    10th Royal Hussars.
    Canadian Light Horse.
    1 Section Canadian Field Artillery.
    1 Section 6th M.G.Squadron (Cavalry).
    6 Heavy Armoured Cars.
    2 Light   do.   do.
    11 Motor Cyclists for inter-communication.

(b) The 2nd Group under Lt.Col. WALKER, D.S.O., consisted of the following:-
    4 Light Armoured Cars.
    Canadian Cyclist Battalion less 1 Platoon.
    5 M.M.G. Batteries.
    20 Motor Cyclist Scouts.
    1 Section Canadian Field Artillery.
    2 Sections Medium Trench Mortars.

(c) The 3rd Group under Lt.Col. MURLING, M.C., consisted of:-
    5 M.M.G. Batteries.
    20 Motor Cyclists.

.....(d).

(d) The Supply Column under Major ARNOLD consisted of the following:-

       1 Motor Lorry.
       1 Supply Lorry.
       1 Ammunition Lorry.
       1 Fuel and Oil Lorry.
       Train of 1st and 2nd C.M.M.G. Brigade.
       5 Motor cyclists for inter-liaison.

4. CONCENTRATION.

The Independent Force was assembled at ZERO (5 a.m. Sept. 2nd) on the WANCOURT - GUEMAPPE Road with the head of the column on the ARRAS - CAMBRAI Road.

The 10th Royal Hussars having bivouacked on the night of Sept. 1st in the valley N.W. of WANCOURT, formed the head of the column together with the 2 Light and 6 Heavy Armoured Cars.

The column was ready to move off at ZERO.

5. ORDER OF MARCH. LEADING GROUP.

       2 Light Armoured Cars.
       6 Heavy   do.   do.
       "A" Sqdn. X.R.H., Capt. the Earl of AIRLIE, M.C.
       1 Section 6th M.G.Squadron.
       1 Squadron Hotchkiss A.R., Canadian Light Horse.
       "B" Sqdn. X.R.H., Capt. R.C.GORDON CANNING, M.C.
       "C" Sqdn. X.R.H., Capt. W.S.MURLAND.
       1 Section Canadian Field Artillery.
       Canadian Light Horse, less H.A.R. Squadron.
       Maltese and Water Carts. Fighting Limber.

6. At ZERO + 3 hours 20 minutes, 8.20 a.m., Lt.Col. WHITMORE received orders to move.

NOTE. In order to save time in the initial stage of the advance, Col. WHITMORE had already moved the Column to a position of readiness with its head at ST.ROHARTS Factory, tail expending parallel to and North of the main CAMBRAI Road, 1500 yards East of the point of assembly referred to in para. 4.

7. The Armoured Cars preceding the Column moved off at once followed by the remainder of the Force. The mounted troops were obliged to keep to the main road the whole way, the land on either side being impassable, until about 2000 yards East of VIS-EN-ARTOIS.

At 9.10 a.m. a verbal message was received from Capt. The Earl of AIRLIE, saying that his leading patrols were up with the Infantry on the RED Line, who could not proceed any further owing to heavy M.G. fire, that the Cross Roads on crest P.26.d.0.2. was being heavily shelled, that the eastern slope of the Hill was being swept by M.G. fire, also that the Armoured Cars were unable to get on on account of strong resistance at the cross roads P.34.d.9.2.

Orders were therefore issued for the patrols to keep in touch with the Infantry and report at once any development. At this time one armoured car (heavy) was reported out of action. The leading Sqdn. 10th Royal Hussars were now distributed in groups on the South of the CAMBRAI Road about P.25.d. together with the 2 subsections 6th M.G. Squadron and Hotchkiss Squadron of the Canadian Light Horse. The remainder of the Leading Group, less section Canadian Field Artillery, on both sides of the road in O.24.d. and O.30.b. 1 Section Canadian Field Artillery was ordered to come into action about P.25.d. against the cemetery P.34.d. and VILLERS LEZ CAGNICOURT. This section remained in action throughout the day.

8. The strong resistance at these two places and also from the direction of the BUISSY SWITCH rendered further advance of Cavalry impracticable until these machine guns had been dealt with, and for this purpose the Medium Trench Mortars were brought into action, firing from their lorries.

........9.

9. In the event of the resistance at the Cemetery and VILLERS LEZ CAGNICOURT being overcome by this bombardment, a further advance by the Leading Group, Independent Force was prepared which involved artillery preparation and support, the purpose of this artillery preparation being as follows:-

    O 10.   East end of VILLERS LEZ CAGNICOURT.
    O 10.   BUISSY SWITCH.
    O 10.   BARALLE WOOD.
    O 60.   SAUDEMONT.
    O 60.   RUMAUCOURT.
    O 60.   Strong point in Q.31.a.

The objective of the Cavalry being to seize the ridge extending in a N.E. direction from about P.12.central to W.2.c. overlooking BARALLE to the S.E. and the GREEN Line to the North.

At 5.0 p.m. the following orders were issued by Lt.Col. WHITMORE to the formations concerned. -

i. "The operations of 2nd Group are progressing favourably which may result in capture of Cemetery and X roads in P.34.d.9.2. and VILLERS CAGNICOURT.

    In this event two Squadrons will attack and seize high ground GIBRALTAR HILL and lane leading from there to V.12.central and spur through W.7.a. & b. & W.2.c.

ii. The Squadrons detailed for the operation will be "B" Squadron, 10th Hussars, under Capt. GORDON CANNING, and 1 Squadron C.L.H. under Major DAWSON; 1 Subsection 6th M.G.Squadron will be attached to each Squadron, one half squadron of Hotchkiss Squadron of C.L.H. will also be attached to each Squadron."

The reconnaissance referred to in above orders was carried out, the result of which caused any further attempt at advance to be abandoned, and the various formations of the Group received orders to withdraw.

The 10th Royal Hussars thereupon marched to WAILLY, where they remained under two hours notice, until orders were received from Cavalry Corps to rejoin the 6th Cavalry Brigade on Sept. 5th.

       Casualties. X.R.H.   1 O.R. wounded.
                             2 O.R. wounded at duty.
                             6 horses.

                              (Sd) F.H.D.C.WHITMORE, Lt.Col.,
10.9.18.   Commanding 10th (P.W.O.) Royal Hussars.

Appendix 3

Reference Map, Sheet LENS 11, 1/100,000.   S E C R E T.

G.S.100/199
9.9.18.

1. Following moves will take place tomorrow, Sept. 10th.

2. (i) H.Q.,R.H.A. 3rd Cavalry Division and Divisional Ammunition Column from WILLEMAN to CAUMONT.
   To be clear of WILLEMAN by 12 Noon.

   (ii) 3rd Field Squadron R.E. from GALAMETZ to CAUMONT.
   To clear GALAMETZ by 12 Noon.

   (iii) Light Section Reserve Park from GALAMETZ to TOLLENT.
   To clear GALAMETZ by 12 Noon.

   (iv) 7th Cavalry Brigade will clear all units from CONCHY-SUR-CANCHE and BOUBERS by 3 P.M. and are allotted GALAMETZ and WILLEMAN instead.
   (N.B. 6th M.G.Squadron are also billeted at WILLEMAN).

3. No restrictions as to routes.

4. On completion of above moves, CONCHY and BOUBERS will be at the disposal of the Canadian Cavalry Brigade for billeting.

5. ACKNOWLEDGE.

9th Sept. 1918.
Issued at 6.30 P.M.

Lieut.Colonel,
G.S., 3rd Cavalry Division.

Copies to:-
  6th Cavalry Brigade.
  7th Cavalry Brigade.
  Canadian Cav. Brigade.
  C.R.H.A.
  A.D.M.S.
  A.D.V.S.
  A.P.M.
  3rd Signal Squadron.
  3rd Fd.Squadron R.E.
  O.C. A.S.C.
  Light Sec. Reserve Pk.
  Heavy Sect. Reserve Pk.

  D.A.C.

  "Q".
  Cav. Corps Adv.
  Cav. Corps "Q".
  Third Army.
  D.M.G.O.

Appendix 14

SECRET.

3rd Cavalry Division Order No.50.

Copy No. 27

Reference Map 1/100,000 LENS Sheet.

14th Sept., 1918.

1.   3rd Cavalry Division (less A.2 and "B" Echelons, Heavy Sections Cavalry Field Ambulances, Heavy Section D.A.C., Light and Heavy Sections 3rd Cavalry Reserve Park, and Aux.H.T.Coy.) will move into the TERNOISE Valley area between HESDIN (exclusive) and BLANGY SUR TERNOISE (inclusive) on Monday, Sept. 16th, in accordance with March Table overleaf.

2.   A map marking Brigade areas "A", "B" and "C", and Divisional Troops area "D.T." is being issued by A.A. & Q.M.G.

3.   A.1 Echelons plus water carts will accompany Brigades and units of Divisional Troops.

4.   Light Sections C.F.A's and Mobile Vet. Sections will accompany Brigades to TERNOISE VALLEY.

5.   On Sept. 17th, the Division, as detailed in para.1, will be concentrated between NOVELLE-LES-HUMIERES and OEUF by 7.30 A.M. Orders for this move will be issued later.

6.   Distances as laid down in S.S.724 will be maintained.

7.   Divisional H.Q. and 3rd Signal Squadron will remain at FONTAINE L'ETALON night 16/17th.

8.   ACKNOWLEDGE.

for Lieut.Colonel,
G.S., 3rd Cavalry Division.

Issued at 6.30 P.M.

Copies to:-
1. 6th Cav. Bde.
2. 7th Cav. Bde.
3. Canadian Cav. Bde.
4. C.R.H.A.
5. 3rd Field Squadron R.E.
6. 3rd Signal Squadron.
7. A.D.M.S.
8. A.D.V.S.
9. A.P.M.
10. "Q"
11. Camp Commandant.
12. } O.C. A.S.C.
13. }
14. D.A.C.
15. Light Sec. Reserve Park.
16. Heavy Sect. Reserve Park.
17. Aux. H.T.Coy.
18. D.M.G.O.
19. Cavalry Corps.
20. 1st Cavalry Division.

March Table issued with 3rd Cavalry Division Order No.50.

Serial No.	Date.	Unit.	Route.	Destination.	Remarks.
1.	Sept. 16th	6th Cavalry Bde.	LE PARCQ.	"A" Area.	To be North of main HESDIN - ST.POL Road by 11.0 A.M.
2.	16th	7th Cavalry Bde.	WILLEMAN - NEULETTE - INCOURT.	"B" Area.	To be North of WILLEMAN by 11.0 a.m.
3.	16th	Canadian Cavalry Brigade.	CROISETTE - BEAUVOIS - HUMIERES - ECLIMEUX.	"C" Area.	To be North of FLERS by 11.0 a.m.
4.	16th	3rd Field Sqdn.	VACQUERIETTE - VIEIL HESDIN.	LE PARCQ - South of main HESDIN - ST. POL Road.	To enter VIEIL HESDIN at 11.0 a.m.
5.	16th	H.Q. 4th Bde.R.H.A. S.A.A.Sect. D.A.C.	As for Serial No.4.	ESTRUVALLE CHATEAU.	To enter VIEIL HESDIN at 11.30 a.m.

Appendix 5

SECRET.

3rd Cavalry Division Order No.53.   Copy No. 17....

Reference Map 1/100,000 LENS Sheet.   17th September, 1918.

1. The following moves will take place today, September 17th, owing to a readjustment of 3rd Cavalry Division billeting area.

2. (a) Light Section Reserve Park from TOLLENT to QUOEUX. - Route via CAUMONT and FONTAINE L'ETALON. - To start at 4 P.M.

   (b) Heavy Section Reserve Park, and Aux. H.T. Company from WILLENCOURT to QUOEUX and HAUT MAISNIL. - Route via VAULX. - To start at 4 P.M.

   (c) Details of H.Q./4th Brigade R.H.A., D.A.C.(less S.A.A. Section), and Divisional H.Q. details now at CAUMONT to VACQUERIETTE and ERQUIERES. - Route via FONTAINE L'ETALON. - To start at 4 P.M. New area to be allotted by O.C., D.A.C.

   (d) Details, 3rd Field Squadron, from CAUMONT to HARAVESNES. - Route via FONTAINE L'ETALON. - To start at 4 P.M.

3. ACKNOWLEDGE.

Lieut.Colonel,
G.S., 3rd Cavalry Division.

Issued at 5 A.M.

Copies to:-
```
   Nos.
   1 - 4.    O.C. A.S.C.
   5 - 6.    A.D.M.S. (1 copy to details at CAUMONT.)
   7 - 8.    4th Brigade R.H.A. (1 copy to details at CAUMONT.)
   9.        D.A.C.
   10 - 11.  3rd Field Squadron. (1 copy to details at CAUMONT.)
   12.       3rd Signal Squadron.
   13.       "Q".
   14.       Cavalry Corps.
   15.       1st Cavalry Division.
```

Appendix 6

SECRET.

Special Instructions for Cavalry Manoeuvres,

September 16th to 17th, 1918.

3rd Cav. Div. No.G.S.215/10 dated 15.9.18.

1. The attached copy of Cavalry Corps instructions is forwarded for information and guidance, together with copies of "General and Special Idea" and "Cavalry Manoeuvres Special Instructions" issued by I.G. Training.

2. <u>Situation at 8 A.M. 17th - Commencement of Operations.</u>

3rd Cavalry Division will be on the line OEUF - NOVELLE-LES-HUMIERES, and not as stated in my G.S.215 dated 11.9.18, para.7 (c).
Orders for move from TERNOISE Valley to above area will be issued later.

3. <u>Ammunition.</u>

10 rounds blank per rifle will be carried and will only be used for occasional shots to indicate that M.G's, Hotchkiss Rifles and Rifles are in action.
A.A. & Q.M.G. will arrange distribution of blank S.A.A. to units as above.

4. <u>Water Carts.</u>

Water carts will accompany units on 16th instant to the area in the TERNOISE Valley.
On the 17th, they will be divisionalized and march with A.1 Echelon, under orders to be issued later.

5. <u>Mess Carts and Officers' Pack Horses.</u>

Mess Carts and Officers' Pack Horses may accompany units to the TERNOISE Valley on 16th instant.
From there on the 17th instant they will be moved forward under Brigade or unit arrangements but no mess cart or Officer's pack horse must cross the Valley of the CANCHE River before 3 p.m.

6. <u>Watering Horses.</u>

All horses must be watered on the morning of the 17th instant before moving from TERNOISE Valley area to the area OEUF - NOVELLE-LES-HUMIERES.

7. <u>Horses.</u>

Such horses as are not considered fit for hard work at once will not be taken out.

8. <u>Dress.</u>

Marching Order, except that Wallets, Horse Bandoliers and Ammunition will be left behind in present billets.
Ball Ammunition in men's bandoliers will be collected and left under Brigade and unit arrangements in present area.
Bandoliers will be worn empty except for 10 rounds blank.

.....9.

-2-

9. **Manoeuvre Area.**

The area is as already stated in G.S.215 of 11.9.18, para. 3.
The following Towns on Rivers CANCHE and AUTHIE will form the East and West boundaries of the Manoeuvre Area. They will be considered impassable and no Troops will pass through them or to the East or West of them respectively.

  River CANCHE. FREVENT, Eastern Boundary.
         HESDIN, Western Boundary.

  River AUTHIE, FROHEN LE GRAND, Eastern Boundary.
         LE BOISLE, Western Boundary.

10. **Umpires.**

The Umpires detailed by 3rd Cavalry Division (i.e. 1 per Cavalry Brigade and 1 per M.G. Squadron) will attend a Conference at the Theatre, AUXI LE CHATEAU, at 3 P.M. on September 16th.
They will also attend a conference at the same place on conclusion of operations.

11. **Liaison and Gallopers.**

Liaison Officers, each with 3 mounted orderlies, will be required with Cavalry Corps and 1st Cavalry Division.
A Galloper, with 4 mounted orderlies, will be required from each Brigade for Divisional H.Q.
Time and place to report for Liaison Officers and Gallopers will be notified later.

12. **Conference at End of Operations.**

On conclusion of operations, Commanding Officers and upwards and all umpires will attend a conference at the Theatre, AUXI LE CHATEAU (behind Town Hall).

13. **Mobile Veterinary Sections.**

Mobile Vet. Sections will accompany Brigades during the operations.

14. **Cavalry Field Ambulances.**

Light Sections C.F.A's will be divisionalized on the 17th inst. under orders to be issued later.

                Lieut.Colonel,
              G.S., 3rd Cavalry Division.

Copies to:-
 6th Cavalry Brigade.
 7th Cavalry Brigade.
 Canadian Cav. Brigade.
 3rd Signal Squadron.
 3rd Field Squadron R.E.
 C.R.H.A.
 "Q".
 A.D.M.S.
 A.D.V.S.
 A.P.M.
 Camp Commandant.
 O.C. A.S.C.
 D.M.G.Q.
 S.A.A.Section, D.A.C.

"A" Form
MESSAGES AND SIGNALS.

Army Form C. 2121
(In pads of 100.)

Appendix 7

TO: 6" Cav Bde, CRHA, ADMS, SAA Sec DAC
7" Cav Bde, Field Sqdn.
Can Cav Bde, Signal Sqdn, A. 1 Echelon

Sender's Number: G.09
Day of Month: 17

AAA

1. Brigades and Divisional Troops will move forthwith into areas in the AUTHIE Valley as follows:-

6" Cavalry Bde - Area C
Route: Any roads S. of MONTIGNY - HEUZECOURT - LE MEILLARD inclusive

7" Cavalry Bde - Area A
Route - Any

Canadian Cav Bde - Area B
Route - T roads 300x N. of last A in AUXI-LE-CHATEAU STA - WAVANS - FROHEN-LE-GRAND - MEZEROLLES

HQ 4" Bde RHA, SAA Sec DAC
3rd Field Sqdn. — WAVANS
Route - Any

3. A.1 Echelons and Light Sections C.F.A's will move to the Northern entrance

"A" Form
MESSAGES AND SIGNALS.

Army Form C. 2121 (In pads of 100.)

	Words	Charge.	This message is on a/c of:	Recd. at......m.
Office of Origin and Service Instructions	Sent			Date...............
	At ....m.		............Service.	From ....
	To			
	By	(Signature of "Franking Officer")	By..............

TO { — 2 —

Sender's Number.	Day of Month.	In reply to Number.	AAA
G 9	17		

to AUXI-LE-CHATEAU on the BUIRE-AU-BOIS — AUXI-LE-CHATEAU Road; Staff Captains will arrange to meet and conduct them to their Brigade areas.

3. 3rd Signal Squadron will return to FONTAINE L'ETALON

4. Divisional HQ will be at FONTAINE L'ETALON

5. Acknowledge

From 3rd Cav Div
Place AUXI-LE-CHATEAU
Time 3.50 pm

Appendix 8

SECRET.

6th Cavalry Brigade.	O.C. A.S.C.
7th Cavalry Brigade.	"Q"
Canadian Cavalry Bde.	A.D.V.S.
C.R.H.A.	A.P.M.
3rd Signal Squadron.	Camp Commandant.
3rd Field Sqdn. R.E.	S.A.A. Sect. D.A.C.
A.D.M.S.	

3rd Cav. Div. G.O.10 dated 17.9.18.

Reference 1/100,000 Sheet LENS 11.

1. 3rd Cavalry Division, now billeted in AUTHIE Valley, will move back on Sept. 18th to billets originally occupied by them in CANCHE Valley on September 14th, with exception of H.Q., 4th Brigade R.H.A., S.A.A. Section D.A.C. and 3rd Field Squadron which billet as shewn below.

   (a) H.Q., 4th Brigade R.H.A. and S.A.A. Section D.A.C. to VACQUERIETTE and ERQUIERES. Route BUIRE AU BOIS, to be North of BUIRE by 8.30 a.m.

   (b) 3rd Field Squadron to HARAVESNES. Head to enter BUIRE AU BOIS at 8.30 a.m.

   (c) 7th Cavalry Brigade to WILLEMAN area, not to cross AUXI - LIGNY SUR CANCHE Road before 8.30 a.m. but to be North of AUXI-DOULLENS Road by 9.30 a.m. No restrictions as to roads.

   (d) Canadian Cavalry Brigade to BOUBERS area, any roads, to be North of BONNIERES by 9.30 a.m.

   (e) 6th Cavalry Brigade to LE PLACITON area. Head of Brigade or Regimental columns to be on AUXI-DOULLENS Road at 9.30 a.m. Brigade to be clear of AUXI-DOULLENS road by 11 a.m.

2. Divisional Headquarters are at FONTAINE L'ETALON.

3. Brigade Areas in CANCHE Valley will be readjusted on Sept. 19th.

4. Staff Captains of Brigades will report to 3rd Cavalry Division "Q" Office between 10 and 11 a.m. September 18th, for new areas.

5. ACKNOWLEDGE.

(Sd) S.G. HOWES, Major,
for Lieut. Colonel,
G.S., 3rd Cavalry Division.

Issued at 6 P.M.

Copy to:- Cavalry Corps.
1st Cavalry Division.

Appendix 9

SECRET.

3rd Cavalry Division Order No.54.   Copy No....

Reference LENS Sheet 1/100,000.   18th September, 1918.

1. The following readjustment of areas will take place on September 19th. (Marked maps shewing areas have been issued to Staff Captains).

(a) 6th Cavalry Brigade from LE PLACITON Area to REBREUVE Area.
Route - WILLEMAN - LINZEUX - BLANGERVAL. To be East of LINZEUX by 12 Noon.
Brigade H.Q. to REBREUVE.

(b) 7th Cavalry Brigade to WILLEMAN area, to redistribute units, giving preference to 6th Cavalry Brigade as regards Roads.
7th Cavalry Brigade H.Q. to remain at WILLEMAN.

(c) Canadian Cavalry Brigade to BOUBERS-SUR-CANCHE Area, to redistribute units, , giving preference to 6th Cavalry Brigade as regards roads.
Canadian Cavalry Brigade H.Q. to BOUBERS-SUR-CANCHE.

(d) Divisional Ammunition Column to FILLIEVRES, North of River CANCHE. Any Roads. Not to start before 2 P.M.

2. Divisional Headquarters remain at FONTAINE L'ETALON.

3. ACKNOWLEDGE.

Issued at 12.30 P.M.

for Lieut.Colonel,
G.S., 3rd Cavalry Division.

Copies to:-
No. 1. 6th Cavalry Brigade.
  2. 7th Cavalry Brigade.
  3. Canadian Cavalry Brigade.
  4. C.R.H.A.
  5. D.A.C.
  6. "Q".
  7. A.D.M.S.
  8. A.D.V.S.
  9. A.P.M.
 10. 3rd Signal Squadron.
 11. 3rd Field Squadron.
 12.)
 13.) O.C. A.S.C.
 14. Camp Commandant.
 15. Cavalry Corps.
 16. Cavalry Corps "G"

Appendix 10

SECRET.
Copy No. 20

3rd Cavalry Division Order No.55.

Reference Map 1/100,000 LENS Sheet.   24th Sept., 1918.

1. The Cavalry Corps (less 2nd Cavalry Division), accompanied by the Mobile 4th Guards Brigade and the Household M.G. Brigade, will be transferred to the Fourth Army and held in G.H.Q. Reserve.

2. In consequence 3rd Cavalry Division will move during night 25/26th September in accordance with March Table overleaf.

3. No movement will take place before 7 P.M. and troops will be in their areas by 6 A.M.

4. Distances as laid down in S.S.724 will be maintained.

5. "A" and "B" Echelons will accompany Brigades and Units of Divisional Troops.

6. Light and Heavy Sections Cavalry Field Ambulances and Mobile Veterinary Sections will accompany Brigades.

7. Divisional H.Q. will close at FONTAINE L'ETALON at 7 P.M., September 25th, and reopen at MARIEUX same hour.

8. ACKNOWLEDGE.

Divn. will move night 26/7 to ALBERT area

H Howits Major
    Lieut.Colonel,
    G.S., 3rd Cavalry Division.

Issued at 6.45 P.M.

Copies to:-
- No. 1. 6th Cavalry Brigade.
- 2. 7th Cavalry Brigade.
- 3. Canadian Cavalry Brigade.
- 4. C.R.H.A.
- 5. 3rd Signal Squadron.
- 6. 3rd Field Squadron R.E.
- 7. "Q".
- 8. A.D.M.S.
- 9. A.D.V.S.
- 10. A.P.M.
- 11.)
- 12.) O.C. A.S.C.
- 13. 3rd Cav. Res. Park.
- 14. Aux. H.T. Coy.
- 15. D.A.C.
- 16. Camp Commandant.
- 17. Cavalry Corps.
- 18. 1st. Cavalry Division.

March Table issued with 3rd Cavalry Division Order No.55.

Serial No.	Date.	Unit.	Starting Point.	Time.	Route.	Destination.	Remarks.
1.	Sept. 25th.	6th Cav. Bde.	LUCHEUX.	10.30 P.M.	PAS.	COUIN – ST.LEGER LES AUTHIE – COIGNEUX – BUS-LES-ARTOIS – LOUVENCOURT.	Troops in BOFFLES & FORTEL to be South of MON LEBLOND by 10 P.M. Bde. H.Q. to billet at LOUVENCOURT.
2.	25th.	Canadian Cav. Bde.	X Rds. just West of MON LEBLOND on PREVENT-DOULLENS Road.	10.30 P.M.	BOUQUEMAISON PAS – LUCHEUX – HALLOY.	PAS – FAMECHON – THIEVRES – AUTHIE.	Brigade H.Q. to billet at AUTHIE.
3.	25th.	7th Cav. Bde.	VACQUERIE-LE-BOUCQ.	10.30 P.M.	BONNIERES – DOULLENS.	HALLOY – CAUMESNIL – BEAUREPAIRE AMPLIER – ORVILLE TERRAMESNIL – SARTON.	Brigade H.Q. to ORVILLE.
4.	25th.	3rd Field Squadron.	WAVANS.	9.0 P.M.	DOULLENS.	VAUCHELLES-LES-AUTHIE.	C.R.H.A. will arrange distribution of billets for Serial Nos. 4 and 5.
5.	25th.	H.Q. 4th Bde. R.H.A.	WAVANS.	10.0 P.M.	DOULLENS.	VAUCHELLES-LES-AUTHIE.	
6.	25th.	Divl. H.Q. 3rd Sig. Sqdn.	WAVANS.	10.15 P.M.	DOULLENS.	MARIEUX.	
7.	25th./26th.	D.A.C.	VACQUERIE-LE-BOUCQ.	12.0 M/N	As for Serial No. 3.	AUTHIEULE.	O.C. A.S.C. will arrange distribution of billets for all units in Serials Nos. 7 and 8.
8.	25th./26th.	H.Q. A.S.C. 3rd Cav.Res. Park. Aux.H.T.Coy.	WAVANS.	12.0 M/N	DOULLENS.	AUTHIEULE.	

Appendix 11

SECRET.

3rd Cavalry Division Order No.56.   Copy No. 25

26th September, 1918.

Reference Map 1/100,000,
LENS & AMIENS Sheets.

1.   3rd Cavalry Division (less units mentioned in para. 6) will move during night 26/27th September to a bivouac area in the ANCRE Valley between DERNANCOURT on the South (exclusive) and HAMEL on the North (inclusive), in accordance with March Table overleaf.
    No troops will bivouac in ALBERT.

2.   "A" and "B" Echelons will accompany Brigades and Units of Divisional Troops.

3.   Light and Heavy Sections Cavalry Field Ambulances and Mobile Veterinary Sections will accompany Brigades.

4.   No movement will take place before 7 P.M. and march will be completed by 6 A.M.

5.   Distances as laid down in S.S.724 will be maintained.

6.   Divisional H.Q. Details, H.Q. A.S.C. and 3rd Signal Squadron will remain at MARIEUX.
    H.Q., 4th Brigade R.H.A. will remain at VAUCHELLES-LES-AUTHIE.

7.   Divisional   Report Centre will remain at MARIEUX.

8.   The Division will move during night 27/28th to an area on the SOMME between CLERY SUR SOMME (exclusive) and CURLU (inclusive).

9.   ACKNOWLEDGE.

                                        Lieut.Colonel,
                                G.S., 3rd Cavalry Division.

Issued at ..7.... A.M.

Copies to:-
    No.1. 6th Cavalry Brigade.
       2. 7th Cavalry Brigade.
       3. Canadian Cavalry Brigade.
       4. C.R.H.A.
       5. 3rd Signal Squadron.
       6. 3rd Field Sqdn.R.E.
       7. "Q".
       8. A.D.M.S.
       9. A.D.V.S.
      10. A.P.M.
      11.)
      12.) O.C. A.S.C.
      13. 3rd Cav. Res. Park.
      14. Aux. H.T. Coy.
      15. D.A.C.
      16. Camp Commandant.
      17. Cavalry Corps.
      18. Cavalry Corps Signals.
      19. Camp Commandant, Cavalry Corps.
      20. O.C. Bridging Park, Cavalry Corps.
      21. 4th Guards Brigade.
      22. 1st Cavalry Division.

March Table issued with 3rd Cavalry Division Order No.56.

Serial No.	Date.	Unit.	Starting Point.	Time.	Route.	Destination	Remarks.
1.	Sept. 26th	6th Cavalry Bde.	FORCEVILLE.	P.M. 9.0.	BOUZINCOURT – ALBERT.	MEAULTE – BECORDEL – BECOURT – FRICOURT.	Units billeted in BUS-LES-ARTOIS & villages North of it; to be South of that place by 9.45 P.M.
2.	26th	Canadian Cavalry Brigade.	BUS-LES-ARTOIS.	P.M. 10.0	BERTRANCOURT – MAILLY-MAILLET	HAMEL – MESNIL – MARTINSART.	
3.	26th	3rd Field Sqdn.	FORCEVILLE.	P.M. 10.30	As for Serial No.1.	ALBERT – DERNANCOURT Road East of R. ANCRE.	
4.	26th	7th Cavalry Bde.	VAUCHELLES-LES-AUTHIE.	P.M. 9.45	LOUVENCOURT – FORCEVILLE.	SENLIS – BOUZINCOURT – AVELUY.	
5.	26th	D.A.C.	As for Serial No.4.	P.M. 11.15	FORCEVILLE – ALBERT.	As for Serial No.3.	
6.	26th	Aux. H.T. Coy. 3rd Cav. Res. Park.	As for Serial No.4.	P.M. 11.45	As for Serial No.5.	As for Serial No.3.	In order of march as in Column 3.

Appendix 12

SECRET.

3rd Cavalry Division Order No.57.   Copy No........

Reference Maps
  1/100,000 - LENS & AMIENS.   27th September, 1918.
  1/40,000 - 62C.

1.   The 3rd Cavalry Division will move during the night September 27/28th to a bivouac area on the R. SOMME between CLERY (exclusive) and CURLU (inclusive) in accordance with March Table attached.
    Brigade and Divisional Troops areas have been allotted to representatives of Brigades and Units.

2.   "A" and "B" Echelons will accompany Brigades and Divisional Troops Units.

3.   Cavalry Field Ambulances and Mobile Veterinary Sections will march with their affiliated Brigades.

4.   Distances as in S.S.724 .

5.   No movement will take place before 7 P.M. and march will be completed by 5.30 A.M.

6.   The Road ALBERT - X roads LE of LE CARCAILLOT - BECORDEL is not to be used by any troops of the Division en route to their Starting Point.

7.   Divisional Report Centre will close at MARIEUX at 5 P.M. 27th and reopen at 2nd S of CLERY SUR SOMME (1/100,000 AMIENS Sheet) at the same hour.

8.   ACKNOWLEDGE.

Issued at ...7 A.M.......

                                  Lieut.Colonel,
                                  G.S., 3rd Cavalry Division.

Copies to:-
  No.1. 6th Cavalry Brigade.
    2. 7th Cavalry Brigade.
    3. Canadian Cav. Brigade.
    4. C.R.H.A.
    5. 3rd Signal Squadron.
    6. 3rd Field Squadron R.E.
    7. "Q".
    8. A.D.M.S.
    9. A.D.V.S.
   10. A.P.M.
   11.)
   12.) O.C. A.S.C.
   13. 3rd Cav. Res. Park.
   14. Aux. H.T. Coy.
   15. D. A. C.
   16. Camp Commandant.
   17. Cavalry Corps.
   18. Cavalry Corps Signals.
   19. Camp Commandant, Cavalry Corps.
   20. O.C. Bridging Park, Cavalry Corps.
   21. 4th Guards Brigade.
   22. 1st Cavalry Division.

March Table issued with 3rd Cavalry Division Order No.57.

Serial No.	Date.	Unit.	Starting Point.	Time to pass S.P.	Route.	Destination. Ref.1/40,000 - 62C.	Remarks.
1.	27th Sept.	6th Cavalry Brigade.	Road junction 800x South of C in CARNOY.	9.45 P.M.	MARICOURT.	B.23.a. & c. - H.10.a & c. - H.4.a. & c. - B.27. - H.3. & 9. - all E. of MAUREPAS-FEUILLERES Road.	(1) Troops are not to use ALBERT-LE CARGAILLOT-BECORDEL Road when proceeding to S.P. (2) Not to debouch on ALBERT-BECORDEL Road before 8 P.M.
2.	27th Sept.	7th Cavalry Brigade.	Road junction at 1st O of BECORDEL - BECOURT.	10.30 P.M.	MARICOURT.	B.26. - H.2. - H.7.b. - H.8. North of SOMME R.	No troops to leave ALBERT on the ALBERT-BECORDEL Road before 8 P.M.
3.	27th Sept.	Canadian Cav. Brigade.	Junction of main PERONNE-ALBERT and BRAY SUR SOMME-ALBERT Roads (S.E.exit of ALBERT).	11.30 P.M.	1st O of BECORDEL-BECOURT-MARICOURT.	B.25. - H.1. - G.6.b. & d. - A.30.d. - all East of MAUREPAS-CURLU Road.	
4.	28th Sept.	Field Squadron. L.A.C. Reserve Park.	As for Serial No.2.	1.30 A.M.	MARICOURT.	A.30. - West of MAUREPAS - CURLU Road.	(1) To march to S.P. via junction of 3 Roads at S.E. exit of ALBERT. (2) Bivouac areas to be allotted by O.C. 3rd Field Squadron. (3) Order of march as in Column 3.
5.	28th Sept.	Aux. H.T.Coy.	As for Serial No.2.	2.15 A.M.	MARICOURT.	H.5.c. - H.11.a	Bivouac area to be allotted by O.C., A.S.C.

P.T.O.

- 2 -

Serial No.	Date.	Unit.	Starting Point.	Time to pass S.P.	Route.	Destination.	Remarks.
6.	27th Sept.	Divisional H.Q. H.Q.,R.H.A. H.Q.,A.S.C. 3rd Signal Sqdn.	Road junction just South of L in LOUVENCOURT	10.30 P.M.	FORCEVILLE - BOUZINCOURT - 1st O of BECORDEL-BECOURT - MARICOURT.	H.4.d.)H.5.c. - H.11.a.	(i) Order of march as in column 3. (ii) Bivouac areas to be allotted by O.C. A.S.C. to R.H.A. H.Q., A.S.C. H.Q., and Signal Sqdn. (iii) Not to enter ALBERT before 1.30 A.M. 28th Sept.

"A" Form
MESSAGES AND SIGNALS.

Army Form C. 2121
(In pads of 100.)

Prefix......Code......m.	Words	Charge.	This message is on a/c of :	Recd. at......m.
Office of Origin and Service Instructions	Sent At ......m. To ...... By		......Service. (Signature of "Franking Officer")	Date...... From ...... By ......

TO | | -2- | | |

Sender's Number.	Day of Month.	In reply to Number.	AAA
G 396	29		

Divisional Starting Point — X roads just N of PERONNE I.21.c & d. Time to pass Div. HQ. 3rd Signal Sqd. HQ RHA, HQ ASC 4 PM AAA C Cavalry Bde 4.15 PM AAA 7 Cavalry Bde 5.15 PM AAA Canadian Cav. Bde 6.15 PM AAA 3rd Field Sqdn. 7.15 PM AAA Divisional A.1 Echelon 7.30 PM AAA Divisional A.2 Echelon 7.45 PM AAA DAC 8.15 PM AAA Light Section Reserve Park 8.30 PM AAA Route AAA PERONNE — DOINGT — X Roads just E of ESTREES-EN-CHAUSSEE Tracks to be used wherever possible AAA "B" Echelon, Heavy Sections C.7.a & Heavy Section Reserve Park will

From			/3-
Place			
Time			

The above may be forwarded as now corrected. (Z)

Censor. Signature of Addressor or person authorised to telegraph in his name
* This line should be erased if not required.

"A" Form
MESSAGES AND SIGNALS.

Army Form C. 2121 (In pads of 100.)

Appendix 13

TO: All concerned

Sender's Number.	Day of Month.	In reply to Number.	AAA
G396	29th		

Reference Map 1/40,000 Sheet 62C

3rd Cav Divn (less "B" Echelon Heavy Section CFA, Aux HT Coy, Heavy Sect Reserve Park) will move today to an area North of the OMIGNON River between BIHECOURT, CAULAINCOURT and POEUILLY all inclusive AAA 9' Corps HQ VERMAND are not to be used AAA Light Section CFA, & MV Section, Mess Carts and Water Carts accompany Bdes and units of Divisional Troops AAA A Echelon will assemble Divl HQ H.4.D 5.30 PM today & march Divisionalized under Major GOODDAY, LSH AAA

"A" Form
MESSAGES AND SIGNALS.

Army Form C. 2121 (In pads of 100.)

| TO | -3- |

Sender's Number.	Day of Month.	In reply to Number.	AAA
G 396	29th		

assemble in area about HEM Station 6.30 PM and be demoralized under Capt JENKINS, T.D.G, whose HQ will be at present 6' Cav. Bde HQ AAA Aux MT Coy will remain in present area AAA Orders regarding subsequent move of Divisional B Echelon Aux MT Coy + Heavy bed Reserve Park will be issued by Cavalry Corps "Q" AAA Distance as laid down in S.S.724 will be maintained AAA Divisional HQ close H. & D. at 7.30 PM. 29" & reopen POEUILLY same hour AAA Acknowledge AAA Addressed all concerned

From 3° Cavalry Division
Place H. & D.
Time 3.30 PM

Sgt. S.G. Howes

SECRET.

Appendix 14

3rd Cavalry Division Order No.58.   Copy No.........

Ref 1/100000 Valenciennes & St Quentin   30th Sept., 1918.

1.   The attacks of the First, Third and Fourth Armies are progressing well. In order to take advantage of the success and to thoroughly exploit it, the 1st and 3rd Cavalry Divisions have been moved to positions of assembly as follows:-

   1st Cavalry Division - head South of ROISEL, tail at BOUCLY, all South of the River OMIGNON.

   3rd Cavalry Division - head at BIHECOURT, tail at CAULAINCOURT, all North of the River OMIGNON.

2.   The 4th Guards Brigade, Household M.G. Brigade (less XVIII Corps Cyclists) remain in their present areas. XVIII Corps cyclists have moved to ALLAINES.

3.   Up to and during the passage of the Cavalry Corps through the Fourth Army, the Cavalry Corps will operate under orders of that Army. Subsequently it will operate independently under orders of G.H.Q.

4.   After passing through the Fourth Army, the role of the Cavalry will be:-

   (a) To move in the general direction of LE CATEAU securing the railway junction at that place and BUSIGNY.

   (b) To operate against the flanks and rear of the enemy opposing our Third and First Armies. During this stage the Cavalry Corps will work in close co-operation with the above mentioned Armies.

   (c) To cut the enemy's communications about VALENCIENNES.

5.   The movement of the Cavalry Corps forward will take place under orders of the Fourth Army, and the following roads will probably be allotted:-

   3rd Cavalry Division.
   BIHUCOURT - VADENCOURT - TUMULUS - BELLENGLISE.

   1st Cavalry Division.
   HERVILLY - Southern edge of HESBECOURT - L.15.a.6.9. - Southern edge of VILLERET - BELLICOURT.

                                             .....Motor Columns

-2-

Motor Columns along the main BRIE - VERMAND Road, and then as for 3rd Cavalry Division.

6. The tasks allotted to Divisions are as follows:-

1st Cavalry Division.

Should the situation be considered favourable for the use of Cavalry, the 1st Cavalry Division will be ordered forward from BELLICOURT by the Cavalry Corps. It will move forward with first objective LE CATEAU. It will secure the railway junction at LE CATEAU, and if the situation permits will move North in the direction of VALENCIENNES, pushing forward detachments to VALENCIENNES to cut the railway communications at that place.

3rd Cavalry Division.

The 3rd Cavalry Division will move forward from BELLENGLISE under orders to be issued by Cavalry Corps. It will follow in reserve, pushing out not less than one Brigade to cover the right rear of the 1st Cavalry Division. Should BUSIGNY Railway junction be not already occupied by our troops, it will secure it until relieved. It will detail one Cavalry Brigade as Corps Reserve which must not be used without reference to Cavalry Corps Headquarters. This Brigade will move along the main BELLENGLISE - MARETZ - LE CATEAU Road.

Both Cavalry Divisions should send out detachments to their left flank to get into touch with the advanced troops of the Third and First Armies, or with the object of heading off detachments of the enemy retreating east.

7. The situation may occur that the BELLENGLISE crossing may not be available. In such a case the 3rd Cavalry Division will follow the 1st Cavalry Division through BELLICOURT, moving up the VADENCOURT - VILLERIT Road.

8. In consequence, 3rd Cavalry Division on moving forward from BELLENGLISE, will follow in reserve the general line of advance of 1st Cavalry Division along the line of ESTREES-MARETZ-LE CATEAU Road, with the 6th Cavalry Brigade covering right rear of 1st Cavalry Division.

9. Tasks are allotted to Brigades as follows:-

........(a)

(a) **6th Cavalry Brigade** will gain touch with and will operate to so as to cover right rear of the 1st Cavalry Division, moving on a general line BRANCOURT - LE - GRAND - BUSIGNY - ESCAUFORT - ST. BENIN - BAZUEL.

Should BUSIGNY Railway junction not be already occupied by our troops, it will secure it until relieved.

(b) **7th Cavalry Brigade** will detail one regiment as left flank guard to Division and to gain touch with advanced troops of First and Third Armies.

Line of advance for flank guard - BEAUREVOIR - ELINCOURT - CLARY - BERTRY - LA SOTIERES.

(c) **Canadian Cavalry Brigade** will be in Corps Reserve but will remain under orders of 3rd Cavalry Division and will move along main BELLENGLISE - MARETZ - LE CATEAU Road.

10. If the crossing at BELLENGLISE is not available and the 3rd Cavalry Division follow 1st Cavalry Division through BELLICOURT, the 6th Cavalry Brigade will push on as rapidly as possible to carry out the role allotted to it in para. 9 (a) above.

Until such time as the 6th Cavalry Brigade are in position, the 1st Cavalry Division will cover its own right with a Brigade, which will be withdrawn into 1st Divisional support so soon as 6th Cavalry Brigade have arrived in position.

Tasks of the 7th and Canadian Cavalry Brigades will remain as in para. 9 (b) and (c) above.

11. No.6 Squadron R.A.F. ("B" Flight) have been given the following mission:-

(a) To keep Division informed of the advance of 1st Cavalry Division.

(b) Of the advance of the First and Third Armies.

(c) Of the movement of enemy reserves and reinforcements up to the line of River OISE and SAMBRE-OISE Canal.

12. If 3rd Cavalry Division moves via BELLENGLISE, Heavy Section D.A.C. and Light Section Reserve Park will move with Division through trench area.

If the 3rd Cavalry Division moves via BELLICOURT behind 1st Cavalry Division, Heavy Section D.A.C. and Light Section Reserve Park will concentrate about BIHECOURT Station and come under Cavalry Corps control.

.......13.

13. Railways will be interrupted but bridges will not be blown up. Charges should be withdrawn from bridges where such exist.

14. If food for men and horses is found, it will be controlled and used, the supplies in Echelons being kept intact as long as possible.
    Position and approximate estimate of contents of any food dumps found will be at once reported to Divisional H.Q.

15. All telegraph wires East of a North and South line through LE CATEAU will be cut. West of that line only those running North and South will be cut.

16. On the order to move forward from the present area, Divisional Starting Point will be X-roads ½ mile North of P of PONTRU.
    (Reference Map 62C, 1/40,000 X-Roads R.6.c.4.5.).

Order of March.	6th Cavalry Brigade,
	Divisional H.Q.,
	H.Q., R.H.A.
	3rd Signal Squadron.
	7th Cavalry Brigade.
	Canadian Cavalry Brigade.
	3rd Field Squadron R.E.
March to S.P. with Brigades, thence divisionalized under A.D.M.S. & A.D.V.S.	(Divisionalized Field Ambulances. (Divisionalized Mob. Vet. Sections. (
	A.1 Echelon.
	S.A.A. Section D.A.C.
	A.2 Echelon.
If Division crosses by BELLENGLISE.	(D.A.C. (Heavy Section). (Light Section, Reserve Park

If Division crosses by BELLICOURT, D.A.C. (Heavy Section) and Reserve Park (Light Section) will concentrate at BIHECOURT Stn. and come under Cavalry Corps control.

Routes.

(a) For BELLENGLISE via Road Junction at STE HELENE.
(b) " PELLICOURT via UI of LE VERGUIER - S.E. of VILLERET.

............17.

17. Divisional Report Centre will be at the head of 7th Cavalry Brigade.

18. ACKNOWLEDGE.

Issued at 11.45 A.M.

                                        Lieut.Colonel,
                             G.S., 3rd Cavalry Division.

Copies to:-
1. 6th Cavalry Brigade.
2. 7th Cavalry Brigade.
3. Canadian Cavalry Brigade.
4. C.R.H.A.
5. 3rd Signal Squadron.
6. 3rd Field Squadron R.E.
7. "Q".
8. A.D.M.S.
9. A.D.V.S.
10. A.P.M.
11.
12. O.C. A.S.C.
13. D.A.C.
14. Light Section, Reserve Park.
15. O.C. A.1 Echelon.
16. O.C. A.2 Echelon.
17. Camp Commandant.
18. Cavalry Corps.
19. No.6 Squadron R.A.F.
20. 1st Cavalry Division.
21. 4th Guards Brigade.
22. Household M.G. Brigade.
23. Lieut.STARKEY, Divisional Observation Section.

"A" Form
MESSAGES AND SIGNALS.

Army Form C. 2121
(In pads of 100.)

Appendix 15

TO: All concerned

Sender's Number: G.414
Day of Month: 30th

AAA

Brigades and Units of Divisional Troops will be at 1½ hours' notice to move on receipt of orders at Brigade and Unit HQ. AAA Acknowledge AAA Added all concerned.

From: 3rd Cavalry Division
Time: 11.45 P.M.

Sd. S.G. Howe
Major

(6339) Wt. W160/M3016 1,500,000 10/17 McA & W Ltd (E1898) Forms W3091.   Army Form W.3091.

Cover for Documents.

Nature of Enclosures.

Notes, or Letters written.

Confidential

War Diary
of
~~General Staff~~
3ᵈ Cavalry Division
Intelligence Summaries
October, 1918

Confidential

War Diary
of
General Staff
3º Cavalry Division
Intelligence Summaries
October 1918

Appendix 1.

SECRET.

3rd Cavalry Division Order No.59.   Copy No. 15

Orders in the event of 3rd Cavalry Division being ordered forward in advance of 1st Cavalry Division to carry out their role.

1. 6th Cavalry Brigade will act as advance guard to the Division and seize the railway junction at LE CATEAU and occupy high ground N.E. and N.W. of LE CATEAU.
   The general line of advance ESTREES - MARETZ - LE CATEAU Road.
   6th Cavalry Brigade will also send a Detachment to interrupt railway communication on LE CATEAU - MAUBEUGE Line as far East as possible.

2. 7th Cavalry Brigade will move in echelon to the right of 6th Cavalry Brigade.
   Line of advance - MONTBREHAIN - BUSIGNY - ST.SOUPLET - BAZUEL.
   If railway communication at BUSIGNY has not been interrupted, 7th Cavalry Brigade will do so and leave a Detachment to secure the railway junction until relieved.
   They will also detail a Detachment to interrupt the railway communication about WASSIGNY.

3. Canadian Cavalry Brigade will move in support along line of ESTREES - MARETZ - LE CATEAU Road, detailing one Regiment as left flank guard, and to keep Division informed of the advance of Third and First Armies.
   General line of advance for flank guard BEAUREVOIR - ELINCOURT - CLARY - BERTRY - LA SOTIERE.

4. Remainder of instructions issued under 3rd Cavalry Division Order No. 58 hold good.

5. Reports to head of Canadian Cavalry Brigade.

6. Acknowledge.

1st Oct., 1918.

Issued at 10 A.M.

Lieut.Colonel,
G.S., 3rd Cavalry Division.

Copies to:-
No. 1 6th Cavalry Bde.
    2 7th Cavalry Bde.
    3 Canadian Cav.Bde.
    4 C.R.H.A.
    5 3rd Signal Squadron.
    6 3rd Field Squadron.
    7 "Q".
    8 A.D.M.S.
    9 A.D.V.S.
   10 A.P.M.
   11. Lieut. CHURCHWARD, R.A.F.
   12 Lieut. STARKEY, Div.Obs.Sec.

"A" Form
MESSAGES AND SIGNALS.

Army Form C. 2121 (in pads of 100).

TO	All Concerned.		
Sender's Number.	Day of Month.	In reply to Number.	AAA
G.427	1st		

Reference para. 4 of 3rd Cavalry Division Order No.60, Division will move tomorrow, 2nd, as ordered AAA Head of Division to be at Starting Point at 09.00 AAA There will be a Conference at Divisional Starting Point at 08.30 tomorrow 2nd Oct. AAA Following will attend:-
Brigadiers and Brigade Majors, O.C. 3rd Field Sqdn., O.C. 3rd Sig.Sqdn., C.R.H.A., A.D.M.S., A.D.V.S., A.P.M., "Q" AAA Acknowledge.

From 3rd Cavalry Division.
Place
Time 23.40

(Sd) G.P.COSENS, Lt.Col.

Appendix 4.

SECRET.

3rd. Cavalry Division Order No. 61.

Copy No.........

Reference 1/100,000 ST. QUENTIN & VALENCIENNES.
1/40,000, Sheets 62B and C.

2nd. October, 1918.

1. The success gained by IX Corps will be exploited at dawn on 2nd October by 5th Cavalry Brigade supported by Infantry in direction of FRESNOY-LE-GRAND - MONTEREHAIN - WIENCOURT.

2. The Cavalry Corps (less 2nd Cavalry Division) will be prepared to advance and carry out the mission as stated in 3rd Cavalry Division Order No.58.

3. The 3rd Cavalry Division will lead and carry out the mission laid down for the 1st Cavalry Division in 3rd Cavalry Division Order No.58. In carrying out this mission it will pass South of JONCOURT.
    The 1st Cavalry Division will be prepared to support 3rd Cavalry Division, carrying out role allotted to 3rd Cavalry Division in 3rd Cavalry Division Order No.58.

4. So soon as the high ground running from FRESNOY-LE-GRAND - BRANCOURT-LE-GRAND - WIENCOURT has been made good, orders will be issued by Cavalry Corps for 1st and 3rd Cavalry Divisions to move and carry out their allotted tasks.

5. In consequence, the 3rd Cavalry Division will move on October 2nd so as to cross by BELLENGLISE Bridge and by 10 A.M. will be echeloned along BELLENGLISE - VADENCOURT Road and clear of it, with head just West of Canal.

6. After passing across Canal, 6th Cavalry Brigade (with 1 Field Troop R.E. attached) will act as advanced guard to Division and seize railway junction at LE CATEAU and occupy high ground N.E. and N.W. of LE CATEAU.

    General line of advance:- South of JONCOURT - South of BRANCOURT LE
                                GRAND - thence N.E. on to line of main
                                MARETZ - LE CATEAU Road.

    First bound:- high ground South of HONNECHY and MAUROIS.

    It will send detachment to interrupt Railway Junction between BUSIGNY and HONNECHY as early as possible.

7. 7th Cavalry Brigade, with 1 Field Troop R.E., will move in echelon to the right of 6th Cavalry Brigade -

    Line of advance:- BECQUIGNY - ESCAUFORT - ST. BENIN.

    First bound:- high ground South and North of BECQUIGNY, East and
                    North of BUSIGNY.

    If railway communication at BUSIGNY has not been interrupted, 7th Cavalry Brigade will do so and leave a detachment to secure railway junction till relieved.

8. Canadian Cavalry Brigade will move in Divisional Support -

    General line of advance as for 6th Cavalry Brigade,-

and will detail one Regiment as left flank guard and to keep Division informed of advance of Third and First Armies.

.........9.

"A" Form
MESSAGES AND SIGNALS.

Army Form C. 2121

TO	All concerned.		
Sender's Number. G.435.	Day of Month. 2nd	In reply to Number.	AAA

Brigades and Units of Divisional Troops will be saddled up in their present bivouac areas and ready to move at 08.30 tomorrow 3rd Oct. AAA Acknowledge AAA Addsd all concerned.

From 3rd Cavalry Division.
Place
Time 19.30.

(Sd) G.P.COSENS, Lt.Col.

Appendix 6.

SECRET.

3rd. Cavalry Division Order No. 62.

Copy No. 22

Map Ref: 1/40.000 sheets 62B & C.

2nd. October, 1918.

In the event of the Division being ordered to move up to a forward assembly area with head of the Division at BELLENGLISE, the following will be Brigade and Divisional Troops Areas and Routes thereto.

6th. Cavalry Brigade & 1 Field troop R.E.

to area M.4.a, b, c, between Ste. HELENE - PONTRUET Road and the Canal, South of BELLENGLISE - VERMAND Road.

Route via track as already reconnoitred by 6th. Cavalry Brigade.

7th. Cavalry Brigade & 1 Field Troop R.E.

M.2.c & d.   M.3.c & d.
between Ste. HELENE and the TUMULUS South of BELLENGLISE - VERMAND Road.

Route via main road.

Canadian Cavalry Brigade.

Area R.11.a. R.4.c & d. up valley North of VADENCOURT.

Route via SOYECOURT and R.8.

3rd. Field Squadron (less 2 troops) follow Canadian Cavalry Brigade to Canadian Cavalry Brigade Area.

Divl. H.Q., C.R.H.A., 3rd. Signal Squadron to G.34.

Route via main road.

A.1 & A.2 Echelons.

Area R.21.central between BIHECOURT STATION and BIHECOURT, South of main road.
Os.C. Divl. A.1 & A.2 to meet Echelons of Brigades and Divisional Troops at BIHECOURT STATION.

Route via main road.

Light Sections Cav. Fd. Ambulances & Mobile Vet. Sections.

Area about X-roads R.3.c. clear of main road.

Route via main road.
On arrival to be Divisionalized under A.D.M.S. & A.D.V.S.

S.A.A. Sect.....

<u>S.A.A. Section D.A.C.</u>

Area between BIHECOURT STATION and BIHECOURT in rear of A.1 Echelon.

<u>D.A.C. and Light Section Reserve Park.</u>

Area about BIHECOURT STATION North of main road.

2. Wheels of Fighting troops may march to assembly areas by main road if tracks are not considered good enough.

3. Brigades will spread over whole of area allotted in small groups.

Issued at 21.15
2nd. October, 1918.

H Hods Major
for Lieut-Colonel,
G.S., 3rd. Cavalry Division.

Copies to :-

No.1	6th. Cavalry Brigade.
2	7th. Cavalry Brigade.
3	Canadian Cavalry Brigade.
4	C.R.H.A.
5	3rd. Signal Squadron.
6	3rd. Field Squadron. R.E.
7	"Q".
8	A.D.M.S.
9	A.D.V.S.
10	A.P.M.
11) 12)	O.C. A.S.C.
13	D.A.C.
14	Light Section Reserve Park.
15	O.C. Divl. A.1 Echelon.
16	O.C. Divl. A.2. Echelon.
17	Camp Commandant.
18	Cavalry Corps.

Appendix 6.

SECRET.

3rd. Cavalry Division Order No. 62.

Copy No...... 22

Map Ref: 1/40,000 sheets 62B & C.

2nd. October, 1918.

In the event of the Division being ordered to move up to a forward assembly area with head of the Division at BELLENGLISE, the following will be Brigade and Divisional Troops Areas and routes thereto.

6th. Cavalry Brigade & 1 Field troop R.E.

to area M.4.a, b, c, between Ste. HELENE - PONTRUET Road and the Canal, South of BELLENGLISE - VERMAND Road.

Route via track as already reconnoitred by 6th. Cavalry Brigade.

7th. Cavalry Brigade & 1 Field Troop R.E.

M.2.c & d.   M.3.c & d.
between Ste. HELENE and the TUMULUS South of BELLENGLISE - VERMAND Road.

Route via main road.

Canadian Cavalry Brigade.

Area R.11.a. R.4.c & d. up valley North of VADENCOURT.

Route via SOYECOURT and R.8.

3rd. Field Squadron (less 2 troops) follow Canadian Cavalry Brigade to Canadian Cavalry Brigade Area.

Divl. H.Q., C.R.H.A., 3rd. Signal Squadron to G.34.

Route via main road.

A.1 & A.2 Echelons.

Area R.21.central between BIHECOURT STATION and BIHECOURT, South of main road.
Os.C. Divl. A.1 & A.2 to meet Echelons of Brigades and Divisional Troops at BIHECOURT STATION.

Route via main road.

Light Sections Cav. Fd. Ambulances & Mobile Vet. Sections.

Area about X-roads R.5.c. clear of main road.

Route via main road.
On arrival to be Divisionalized under A.D.M.S. & A.D.V.S.

S.A.A. Scot.....

S.A.A.Section D.A.C.

    Area between BIHECOURT STATION and BIHECOURT in rear of A.1 Echelon.

D.A.C. and Light Section Reserve Park.

    Area about BIHECOURT STATION North of main road.

2.   Wheels of Fighting troops may march to assembly areas by main road if tracks are not considered good enough.

3.   Brigades will spread over whole of area allotted in small groups.

Issued at 21.15
2nd. October, 1918.

                              J H Hooks Major
                                      for Lieut-Colonel,
                             G.S., 3rd. Cavalry Division.

Copies to :-

No.1	6th. Cavalry Brigade.
2	7th. Cavalry Brigade.
3	Canadian Cavalry Brigade.
4	C.R.H.A.
5	3rd. Signal Squadron.
6	3rd. Field Squadron. R.E.
7	"Q".
8	A.D.M.S.
9	A.D.V.S.
10	A.P.M.
11) 12)	O.C. A.S.C.
13	D.A.C.
14	Light Section Reserve Park.
15	O.C. Divl. A.1 Echelon.
16	O.C. Divl. A.2 Echelon.
17	Camp Commandant.
18	Cavalry Corps.

"A" Form
MESSAGES AND SIGNALS.

Army Form C. 2121
(in pads of 100).

TO: Canadian Cavalry Brigade.

Sender's Number.	Day of Month.	In reply to Number.	AAA
G.C.510	3rd		

Move back your Brigade at once to the area occupied by 7th Cavalry Brigade last night, i.e. N. and W. of VERMAND AAA Divisional H.Q. are returning to POEUILLY later but will remain at TUMULUS Cavalry Corps Report Centre for the present.

From 3rd Cavalry Division.
Place
Time 17.45

(Z) (Sd) G.P.COSENS, Lt.Col.

"A" Form
MESSAGES AND SIGNALS.

Army Form C. 2121
(in pads of 100).

TO: 7th Cavalry Brigade.

Sender's Number.	Day of Month.	In reply to Number.	AAA
G.C.511	3rd		

Move your Brigade back at once to the area occupied by 6th Cavalry Brigade last night i.e. about BIHECOURT and BIHECOURT Station and N.E. outskirts of VERMAND AAA Canadian Cavalry Brigade are going back to the area occupied by you last night W. of VERMAND AAA Divisional Report Centre returning to POEUILLY later but will remain at the TUMULUS for the present AAA Acknowledge.

From: 3rd Cavalry Division.
Place:
Time: 17.50.

(Sd) G.P.COSENS Lt.Col.

"A" Form
MESSAGES AND SIGNALS.

Army Form C. 2121 (in pads of 100).

TO	All concerned.		
Sender's Number. G.C.520	Day of Month. 3rd	In reply to Number.	AAA

Division (less 6th Cavalry Brigade) will be at four hours notice until further orders AAA Addressed all concerned.

From 3rd Cavalry Division.
Place TUMULUS M.1.d.
Time 20.05.

(Sd) G.P.COSENS, Lt.Col.

Appendix 11

SECRET.
Copy No. 17

3rd Cavalry Division Order No.63.

Reference 1/40,000 Sheets 62B and 62C.   5th October, 1918.

1. 6th Cavalry Brigade (less Brigade A.2 Echelon and Squadron detached at H.19.b.) and 1 Troop, 3rd Field Squadron R.E. attached will move from STE. HELENE area to TREFCON today, October 5th. March to be completed by 3 P.M.

    Route - across country to BIHECOURT, thence South of OMIGNON River.

    Distances as laid down in S.S.724 to be maintained.

2. Rations and forage will be issued in TREFCON area.

3. Orders regarding detached Squadron will be issued separately.

4. ACKNOWLEDGE.

    Lieut.Colonel,
    G.S., 3rd Cavalry Division.

Issued at 07.00.

Copies to:-
    No.1. 6th Cavalry Bde.
       2. 7th Cavalry Bde.
       3. Canadian Cav. Bde.
       4. C.R.H.A.
       5. 3rd Field Squadron, R.E.
       6. 3rd Signal Squadron.
       7. A.D.M.S.
       8. A.D.V.S.
       9. A.P.M.
      10. "Q".
      11. O.C. A.S.C.
      12. Camp Commandant.
      13. Cavalry Corps.
      14. IX Corps.

Appendix 12.

SECRET.
Copy No. 33

3rd Cavalry Division Order No.64.
(ALL PREVIOUS ORDERS ARE CANCELLED).

Reference Maps:
1/40,000 Sheets 62B & C.   6th October, 1918.

1. The Third and Fourth Armies will attack the German Armies opposed to them on Z day.

2. The general directions given for the attacks are:-

   Third Army in the general direction of CAUDRY.
   Fourth Army in the general direction of BOHAIN.

3. Boundaries between Corps and Armies, and objectives given to Infantry Corps are as given at the Conference today, on map issued to G.Os.C. Brigades.

4. The First French Army will attack with objective the line ESSIGNY LE PETIT, FONTAINE UTERTE, and if successful will exploit East of that line.

5. The task of the Cavalry Corps is:-

   (a) To move in the general direction of LE CATEAU, securing the railway junction at that place and BUSIGNY.
   (b) To operate against the flank and rear of the enemy opposing our Third and First Armies. During this stage the Cavalry Corps will work in close co-operation with the above-mentioned Armies.
   (c) To cut the enemy's communications about VALENCIENNES.

6. In order to carry out the above mission, the 1st Cavalry Division will be the leading Division, and will keep in close touch with the advance of the American and XIII Corps. If their advances are successful, and if after reaching their line of exploitation including the villages of PREMONT and SERAIN, reports show that the enemy are demoralized and that their organized resistance has been broken down, the 1st Cavalry Division will advance to carry out the instructions issued in para. 5. Its first main objective should be the high ground W. and S.W. of LE CATEAU, so as to deny the roads and railways running through LE CATEAU to the enemy, and the latter and all telegraph wires should be cut as soon as possible. The LE CATEAU - BUSIGNY Line will be interrupted as soon as possible.
   Should the situation then permit, the high ground North and East of LE CATEAU should be occupied and preparations made for a further advance in the direction of VALENCIENNES. The main body of the Division will not advance from LE CATEAU unless ordered to do so by the Cavalry Corps.

   The 3rd Cavalry Division will follow close behind the rear Brigade of the 1st Cavalry Division, and will send troops out to the high ground E. and S. of BUSIGNY and N.W. of MARETZ, so as to protect the right and left rear of the 1st Cavalry Division until relieved by Infantry.
   It will detail one Cavalry Brigade as Corps reserve, which must not be used without reference to Cavalry Corps H.Q. This Brigade will move along the main BELLENGLISE-MARETZ-LE CATEAU Road.
   Whippet tanks will be sent up as early as possible to assist the 3rd Cavalry Division to clear the enemy out of both BUSIGNY and MARETZ if necessary.   and Household M.G.Brigade
   As the Cavalry advance, the 4th Guards Brigade/will be brought forward in their busses across the Canal, and used to relieve or support the Cavalry Divisions as required.
   ....7.

-2-

7.   The 5th Cavalry Brigade under IX Corps are assembling W. of LEHAUCOURT after dark on Y day.
     They will move forward at such an hour on Z day as to enable them to clear the RED Line immediately in rear of the Infantry and Whippet Tanks advancing against 2nd objective.
     They will exploit the success of the Infantry.
     Should the French not reach FONTAINE UTERTE, the bulk of the Brigade will strengthen the Southern flank and assist the French by securing MERICOURT and getting in touch with French.
     Strong patrols to be sent to BOHAIN and SEBONCOURT.
     Further orders will be issued in accordance with the situation.

8.   1st Cavalry Division assembly areas are as follows:-

        9th Cavalry Brigade   ...   ...   H.7.c. & d.
        1st Cavalry Brigade   ...   ...   G.18.c. & d. & G.24.a. & b.
        2nd Cavalry Brigade   ...   ...   G.11.a.
        Divisional Troops   ...   ...   G.10.d. & 16.b.(E. of Canal)

     1st Cavalry Division Report Centre ...   G.18.a.3.3.

9.   In consequence, 3rd Cavalry Division will be concentrated in an assembly area S.W. of JONCOURT by 08.00 on Z day under orders to be issued separately.

10. Tasks are allotted as follows:-

(a) 7th Cavalry Brigade, with 1 Field Troop R.E. attached, will keep in touch with the advance of 1st Cavalry Brigade, and so soon as that Brigade has passed East of BUSIGNY, will move forward and seize the high ground East and South of BUSIGNY so as to protect the right rear of the 1st Cavalry Division until relieved by the Infantry. Patrols to general line REGNICOURT (E.14.a.) - ANDIGNY-LES-FERMES (E.10.b.) - River SELLE.

(b) Canadian Cavalry Brigade, with 1 Field Troop R.E. attached, will keep in touch with advance of 2nd Cavalry Brigade, and so soon as that Brigade has passed East of MARETZ, will move forward and seize the high ground North-West of MARETZ, so as to protect the left rear of 1st Cavalry Division until relieved by the Infantry. Patrols to the line SELVIGNY - MONTIGNY - TROISVILLES.

(c) 6th Cavalry Brigade will be in Corps Reserve but will remain under orders of 3rd Cavalry Division.
    It will detail one Squadron to act as escort to Cavalry Corps H.Q. which will report so soon as Headquarters, Cavalry Corps are established at ESTREES.

(d) Division, less 7th and Canadian Cavalry Brigades, and 2 Field Troops R.E. will move forward from assembly area along the line of main ESTREES-MARETZ-LE CATEAU Road in order of march as follows:-
        Divisional Headquarters.
        Escort Troop.
        3rd Signal Squadron.
        "D" Battery, 23rd A.F.A. Brigade.
        3rd Field Squadron, less 2 Troops.
        6th Cavalry Brigade.
        A.1 Echelon Divisionalized.
        S.A.A. Section D.A.C.

........11.

-5-

11. No.6 Squadron R.A.F. ("B" Flight) will report as follows:-

   (a) If BUSIGNY and MARETZ are held by the enemy.
   (b) On the progress of advance of 1st Cavalry Division after passing line BUSIGNY-MARETZ.

12. Railways will be interrupted but bridges will not be blown up. Charges should be withdrawn from bridges where such exist.

13. All telegraph wires will be cut.

14. RED Ground Flares will be used and also Cavalry Corps Parachute Signal.

15. If food for men and horses is found, it will be controlled and used, the supplies in the Echelons being kept intact as long as possible.
    Position and approximate estimate of contents of any food dumps found will be reported at once to Divisional H.Q.

16. Communications. Wireless will be put up at Headquarters of Formations at ZERO Hour, but no key will be pressed until 09.00.
    A.D.Signals, Cavalry Corps, will be prepared to lay a cable forward from ESTREES along the road to MARETZ as early as possible after the Infantry advance.

17. Field Ambulances and Mobile Veterinary Sections will be Divisionalized and orders will be issued as situation develops.

18. A.2 Echelon will be Divisionalized and move under orders of A.A.& Q.M.G.

19. Heavy Section D.A.C. and Light Section Reserve Park will remain in present area about BIEFCOURT Station and will come under Corps control.

20. Brigades will make a special point of sending back reports regarding the roads, with a view to the passage of lorries.

21. Divisional Report Centre will be established at ZERO Hour at TUMULUS M.1.d., moving thence to H.19.b. on JONCOURT-BELLENGLISE Road.
    On moving forward from assembly area, so far as can be foreseen at present, it will be at the N.E. end of ESTREES.

22. ACKNOWLEDGE by wire.

Issued at 18.00.

                              Lieut.Colonel,
                        G.S., 3rd Cavalry Division.

Copies to:- No.1 6th Cav. Bde.
          2 7th Cav. Bde.
          3 Candn.Cav.Bde.
          4 3rd Field Sqdn.R.E.
          5 3rd Signal Squadron
          6 C.R.H.A.
          7 "Q"
          8 A.D.M.S.
          9 A.D.V.S.
         10 A.P.M.
      11&12 O.C. A.S.C.
         13 D.A.C.

No.14 Light Sect.Reserve Pk.
    15 O.C.Div.A.1 Echelon.
    16 O.C.Div.A.2 Echelon.
    17 Camp Commandant.
    18-19 No.6 Squadron R.A.F.
        (Liaison Officer).
    20 Cavalry Corps
    21 1st Cavalry Divn.
    22 Lieut.STARKEY,Div.Obs.
        Section.
    23 5th Cavalry Bde.
    24 4th Guards Bde.
    25 Household M.G.Bde.
    26 17th Armoured Car Batt

Appendix B

SECRET.

3rd Cavalry Division Order No.65.   Copy No...24..

Reference Map:
1/40,000 Sheets 62C & 62B.   6th October, 1918.

1. A.1 and A.2 Echelons of Brigades and Divisional Troops, Light Sections Cavalry Field Ambulances and Mobile Veterinary Sections will be divisionalized tomorrow afternoon, October 7th, in the area just East and West of PONTRUET - STE.HELENE Road (Squares M.4 and M.3.) South of main BEILENGLISE-VERMAND Road.

2. Echelons and Light Sections C.F.As. and Mobile Veterinary Sections will march to above area under Brigade and Unit arrangements so as to arrive on PONTRUET - STE.HELENE Road between 16.00 and 17.00 hours.
   6th Cavalry Brigade Echelon, Field Ambulance and Mobile Vet. Section will move South of OMIGNON River.

3. Os.C. Divisionalized A.1 and A.2 Echelons and representatives of Divisionalized Field Ambulances and Mobile Veterinary Sections to be detailed by A.D.M.S. and A.D.V.S. respectively will meet a Divisional Staff Officer at ST.HELENE X-roads at 12.00 hours, October 7th, in order to be allotted areas.

(X)
5. ACKNOWLEDGE.

[signature] Major,
G.S., 3rd Cavalry Division.

Issued at 19.00....

Copies to:-
No.1	6th Cavalry Bde.	No.10	"Q"
2	7th Cavalry Bde.	11,12	O.C. A.S.C.
3	Canadian Cav. Bde.	13	D.A.C.
4	3rd Field Squadron.	14	Camp Commandant.
5	3rd Signal Squadron.	15	O.C.Div.A.1 Echelon. (Capt.ALSOP.)
6	C.R.H.A.		
7	A.D.M.S.	15	O.C.Div.A.2 Echelon (Major GOODDAY)
8	A.D.V.S.		
9	A.P.M.	16	Cavalry Corps.
		17	IX Corps.

4. S.A.A. Section D.A.C. will move to area as in para.1 tomorrow afternoon, October 7th, and will park next to Divisionalized A.1 Echelon.
   O.C. S.A.A. Section to meet Divisional Staff Officer at STE. HELENE X-roads at 12.00.

Appendix 114

S E C R E T.

3rd Cavalry Division Order No. 66.   Copy No.......

Reference Maps:
1/40,000 Sheets 62C & 62B.   7th October, 1918.

1. 3rd Cavalry Division (less "B" Echelon, Heavy Sections Cavalry Field Ambulances and Heavy Section Reserve Park) will be assembled on Z day by 08.00 hours in accordance with March Table overleaf.

2. Z day will be notified later.

3. The following distances only will be maintained; i.e. 50 yards between every 2 troops and Sections of Batteries and Sections of Machine Gun Squadrons and between groups of 12 vehicles.

4. Brigades and Units of Divisional Troops on arrival in their assembly area will establish their report centres on the JONCOURT.-BELLENGLISE Road.

5. Divisional Report Centre as in Order No.64, para. 21, of October 6th.

6. ACKNOWLEDGE.

(Sd) S.G.HOWES, Major, for
Lieut.Colonel,
Issued at 07.00.   G.S., 3rd Cavalry Division.

Copies to:-
```
No.1  6th Cavalry Brigade.
   2  7th Cavalry Brigade.
   3  Canadian Cavalry Brigade.
   4  3rd Field Squadron.R.E.
   5  3rd Signal Squadron.
 6-7  C.R.H.A.(Copy for "D" Battery 23rd Bde. A.F.A.).
   8  A.D.M.S.
   9  A.D.V.S.
  10  A.P.M.
  11  "Q".
  12  Light Section Reserve Park.
 13)
 14)  O.C. A.S.C.
  15  D.A.C.
  16  S.A.A.Section D.A.C.
  17  Camp Commandant.
 18)
 19)  IX Corps.
  20  1st Cavalry Division.
  21  5th Cavalry Brigade.
  22  No.6 Squadron R.A.F.Liaison Officer.
  23  Cavalry Corps.
  24  O.C. Divisionalized A.1 Echelon.
```

March Table issued with 3rd Cavalry Division Order No.66.

Serial No.	Date.	Unit.	Starting Point.	Time.	Route.	Assembly Area	Remarks.
1.	Z Day	7th Cav. Bde. + 1 troop 3rd Field Squadron.	Any.	—	South of OMIGNON River - MAISSEMY - PONTRUET - Canal Bridge M.5.b.8.1. - X Roads LA BERGERE - X Roads H.31.b.	H.15.c., H.14.d., H.20.	To be East of MAISSEMY by 05.00 & East of Canal by 06.30.
2.	do.	Canadian Cavalry Bde + 1 troop 3rd Field Sqdn.	X Roads R.6.c.	04.00	X Roads STE.HELENE - Canal Bridge G.34.d.5.7. - LA BARAQUE.	H.14.a.,b.,&c., H.13.b. & d.	To be East of BELLENGLISE Bridge by 06.00.
3.	do.	6th Cavalry Bde.	Road junction X.2.b.7.7. S. of MARTEVILLE.	04.30	South of OMIGNON River - PONTRUET - Canal Bridge M.5.b.8.1. - X Roads, LA BERGERE.	G.30.c. & d. G.36.a. & b.	
4.	do.	3rd Field Sqdn. less 2 Troops.	As for Serial No.2.	05.00	As for Serial No.2.	H.19.c. S. of JONCOURT Road.	To be East of BELLENGLISE Bridge by 06.15.
5.	do.	"D" Battery 23rd Bde. A.F.A.	do.	05.15	do.	H.19.a.	
6.	do.	Divl.H.Q.Details. 3rd Signal Sqdn. H.Q. R.H.A.	do.	05.30	do.	H.19.b. N. of JONCOURT Road	
7.	do.	Divisionalized Light Sections Cav.Fd.Ambces.	Canal Bridge G.34.d.5.7.	06.30	LA BARAQUE	G.30.b.	Under orders of A.D.M.S.
8.	do.	Divisionalized Mob.Vet.Sections	As for Serial No.7	06.45	do.	G.30.b.	Under orders of A.D.V.S.
9.	do.	Divisionalized A.1 Echelon.	do.	07.00	do.	G.30.a. S. of JONCOURT Road	
10.	do.	S.A.A.Section D.A.C.	do.	07.15	do.	As for Serial No.9	Follow and park with A.1 Echelon.

Appendix 15

SECRET.

ADDENDA TO 3RD. CAVALRY DIVISION ORDER NO. 64.

Copy No. 35

Ref: Maps. 1/40,000 62B & C.

7th. October, 1918.

1. So soon as 9th. Cavalry Brigade have passed through the Infantry, Brigade Headquarters will fire a rocket of golden rain from about C.13. or C.7.

2. The Infantry will be ordered to push forward to BUSIGNY and MARETZ after they have reached the GREEN LINE.

3. The 9th. Cavalry Brigade are assembling in B.28.a. & b. by 07.30.

4. The 5th. Cavalry Brigade has as objective the high ground West and South of BOHAIN.

5. Six Whippet Tanks have been allotted to 1st. Cavalry Division.

6. In the event of the woods W. of BUSIGNY being held, the 1st. Cavalry Division will pass to the North of them and the 7th. Cavalry Brigade will contain them until arrival of the Infantry, passing one Regiment forward to the North of BUSIGNY to hold the high ground E. of that place and also to protect the right rear of 1st. Cavalry Division.

7. Canadian Cavalry Brigade with 1 Field Troop R.E. attached will keep in touch with 1st. Cavalry Division (the Brigade moving N. of ESTREES - LE CATEAU Road i.e. 2nd. Cavalry Brigade) and so soon as that Brigade has passed E. of MARETZ will detail one Regiment to seize the high ground N.W. of that place, so as to protect the left rear of 1st Cavalry Division until relieved by Infantry.
    It will keep two Regiments as Divisional Reserve which will move forward under orders of G.O.C. Canadian Cavalry Brigade, but will not be used without orders from the Division.
    Patrols to the line CLARY - BERTRY - TROISVILLES.

8. Tracks forward from assembly area over Trench line have been made and wire cut.
    They run as follows:-

(a) From about H.8.d.2.8. - H.3.c.0.0. - H.4.a.0.0. to near N.W. exit of VIANCOURT.

.........(b)

"A" Form
MESSAGES AND SIGNALS.

Army Form C. 2121
(In pads of 100.)

This message is on a/c of: Appendix 16

TO All concerned.

Sender's Number.	Day of Month.	In reply to Number.	
G.C.21	8th		AAA

Division will withdraw at once and bivouac for the night as follows:- 6th Cavalry Bde. Valley S.W. of MAGNY LA FOSSE H.25.c. G.30 & 36, between BELLENGLISE-JONCOURT and BELLENGLISE-LEVERGIES Roads AAA 7th Cavalry Bde. and 1 Field Troop R.E. in Squares G.18, 23, 24, 29.a. & b. including ETRICOURT AAA Canadian Cavalry Brigade and 1 Field Troop area about BELLECOURT and NAUROY both inclusive Squares G.10.b. & d., G.11., G.12.a. & c., G.17., all North of main ESTREES road AAA 3rd Field Squadron (less 2 Troops) in 6th Cavalry Bde. area (to be arranged with Brigade) AAA A.1 Echelon and S.A.A.Section D.A.C. to area G.36.d. S. of BELLENGLISE - LEVERGIES Road AAA "D" Batt. 23rd Bde. A.F.A. to area G.35.cent. W. of main BELLECOURT - ST.QUENTIN Road AAA A.2 Echelon & Light Section

/2

"A" Form
MESSAGES AND SIGNALS.

Army Form C. 2121 (In pads of 100.)

TO — 2 —

Sender's Number: G.G.21

AAA

Reserve Park will remain in present area just S.W. of JONCOURT AAA Divisional H.Q., H.Q. R.H.A 3rd Signal Squadron to MAGNY LA FOSSE.

All troops will keep off the road when marching back AAA Field Ambulances and Mob. Vet. Sections will rejoin Brigades in above areas AAA Heavy Section D.A.C. will remain in present position at G.34.d. AAA Divisional H.Q. to Church at MAGNY LA FOSSE.

From: 3rd Cavalry Division.
Place:
Time: 16.45

(Sd.) G.P. COSENS, Lt. Col.,

"A" Form
MESSAGES AND SIGNALS.

Army Form C. 2121
(In pads of 100.)

TO: All concerned.

Sender's Number.	Day of Month.	In reply to Number.	AAA
G.C.25.	8th		

Warning Order AAA Attack will continue tomorrow 9th Oct. and 3rd Cavalry Division will be leading Division AAA Early start probable AAA Orders will be sent as soon as possible after receipt from Cavalry Corps AAA Brigadiers will be required to attend Divisional H.Q. at an hour to be notified later.

From: 3rd Cavalry Division.
Place: H.19.b.
Time: 20.00

(Z) (Sd) G.P.COSENS, Lt.Col.

SECRET.

3rd Cavalry Division Order No.70.

9th October, 1918.

1. The Fourth Army will continue its attack this morning at 05.20.

2. Objectives as follows:-

1st Objective:

XIII Corps	... ...	ELINCOURT - AVELU - MARETZ.
2nd American Corps	...	Wood V.13, 14, 19, 20, 26, 27, and in D1, 2 and 3.
IX Corps	... ...	FRESNOY - Road between FRESNOY and BOHAIN.

2nd Objective.

XIII Corps	... ...	MAUROIS - HONNECHY.
2nd American Corps	...	BUSIGNY - PECQUIGNY.
IX Corps	... ...	BOHAIN.

3. The role of Cavalry Corps is to keep in close touch with the advancing Infantry and to take advantage of any success to move forward to its objective which remains the same as yesterday.

4. The 3rd Cavalry Division will lead and by 07.00 will be in a position of readiness in the valley running from BRANCOURT to VAUX-le-PRETRE FME. C.14.b. in accordance with orders already issued.

5. In order to carry out the above mission the 3rd Cavalry Division with 17th Armoured Car Battalion will keep in close touch with the advance of American and XIII Corps. If the advance of these Corps is successful and if, after reaching 2nd objective, reports shew that the enemy are demoralised and that their organised resistance has been broken down, the 3rd Cavalry Division will advance on its objective.

(a) The high ground W. and S.W. of LE CATEAU so as to deny to enemy the roads and railways running through LE CATEAU. Railways and all telegraph wires will be cut as soon as possible.

(b) Should the situation then permit, the high ground N. and E. of LE CATEAU will be occupied and preparations made for a further advance on VALENCIENNES. The main body of 3rd Cavalry Division will not advance from LE CATEAU unless ordered to do so by Cavalry Corps.

6.(a) 1st Cavalry Division will closely support 3rd Cavalry Division and will be concentrated in the area between MONTBREHAIN, and BEAUREVOIR by 08.00.

(b) The Household M.G. Brigade will be ready to move 1 Battalion in support of 3rd Cavalry Division after 08.00.

7. In consequence, when the Infantry of the American and XIII Corps have gained their objectives, they will be closely followed by 7th Cavalry Brigade who will advance and seize their objective if the situation is as described in para. 5.

8. On orders to 3rd Cavalry Division to carry out allotted task, the Division will move as follows:-

.......(a)

- 2 -

(a) 7th Cavalry Brigade and 1 Field Troop R.E. and 3 Armoured Cars as Advanced Guard. General line of advance ESTREES - LE CATEAU Road.

(b) 6th Cavalry Brigade and 1 Field Troop R.E. on right will detail one Regiment as right flank guard to Division.

(c) Canadian Cavalry Brigade on left will detail one Regiment as left flank guard to Division.

(d) Main bodies of 6th and Canadian Cavalry Brigades will move in echelon of 7th Cavalry Brigade S. and N. respectively of and parallel to main ESTREES - LE CATEAU Road and on general line about 600 to 800 yards from the road. At least one Cavalry Regiment from each of these 2 Brigades will be kept in hand to act as Divisional Reserve.

(e) Divisional H.Q. and Divisional Troops in order of march as under will move on a general line main ESTREES - LE CATEAU Road.

    Escort troops as advanced guard.
    1 Section Armoured Cars.
    Divisional H.Q.
    3rd Signal Squadron.
    "D" Battery, 23rd A.F.A.Brigade.
    3 Field Squadron less 2 Troops).
    A.1 Echelon Divisionalized.
    S.A.A.Section, D.A.C.

First Bound.

7th Cavalry Brigade: Ridge N. of LE CATEAU astride the CAMBRAI - LE CATEAU Road, Point 100, spurs commanding crossings of SELLE River at MONTAY - SELLE Valley S. of NEUVILLY to about RAMBOURLIEUX FME.

6th Cavalry Brigade: Spurs overlooking valley between LE CATEAU (in touch with right of 7th Cavalry Brigade) and ST. BENIN (incl.). 6th Cavalry Brigade will send a special detachment as early as possible to secure and cut railways about Station between LE CATEAU and ST. BENIN.

Canadian Cavalry Brigade: (in touch with left of 7th Cavalry Brigade about RAMBOURLIEUX FME) Cross Roads N.E. of LA SOTIERE covering all approaches in an E. and S.E. direction from TROISVILLES.

9. Instructions re employment of Armoured Cars will be issued separately.

10. "B" Flight, No.6 Squadron R.A.F. will co-operate with the Division and carry out special reconnaissances as under:-

(a) Ascertain whether high ground N. and N.E. of ERS is clear of enemy.

(b) To report on advance of our own Infantry.

(c) To ascertain situation of advanced troops of Third Army on our left.

11. Divisional Report Centre in Farm C.7.a. and as advance progresses along ESTREES-LE CATEAU Road.

(Sd) G.P.COSENS, Lt.Col.,
G.S., 3rd Cavalry Division.

H.19.b.
Issued at 04.00.

Appendix No 9

"A" Form
MESSAGES AND SIGNALS.

Army Form C. 2121
(In pads of 100.)

TO	All concerned.

Sender's Number.	Day of Month.	In reply to Number.	AAA
G.C.27	9th		

1. Divn. will concentrate as follows today.
2. Divl. H.Q. and 3rd Field Squadron at C.7.c. by 05.30 hours.

    7th Cav. Bde. +1 Field Troop about C.8.c. by 06.00 hours.

    Canadian Cav. Bde. +1 Field Troop about C.1.c. by 06.00 hours.

    6th Cav. Bde. about B.12.a. & c. by 07.00 hours.

    "D" Batty. 23rd A.F.A.Bde. in rear of 6th Cav. Bde. in B.12.c. by 07.00 hours.

    3rd Field Squadron less 2 troops in B.18.a. by 07.00 hours.

    A.1 Echelon and S.A.A.Sect. D.A.C. in rear of Field Squadron B.18.a. by 07.00 hours.

ROUTES. 7th Cav. Bde. N. of JONCOURT, N. of WIANCOURT, B.28., B.24.

/2.

"A" Form
MESSAGES AND SIGNALS.

Army Form C. 2121
(In pads of 100.)

Sender's Number.	Day of Month.	In reply to Number.	
G.C.27.	9th		AAA

TO: -2-

Canadian Cav. Bde. along line of main ESTREES - LE CATEAU Road (off road where possible).

6th Cav. Bde., "D" Batty. 23rd A.F.A.Bde., 3rd Field Sqdn., A.1 Echelon, S.A.A.Sect.D.A.C., follow 7th Cavalry Bde.

Divl. H.Q. and 3rd Signal Sqdn. JONCOURT - ESTREES - LE CATEAU Road.

Field Ambces. and Mobile Vet. Sections will be divisionalized and move under orders of A.D.M.S. & A.D.V.S. to vicinity of GENEVE. Route as for Divl. H.Q.

A.2 Echelon, Light Sect. Reserve Park, Heavy Sect. D.A.C. remain in present area.

Divl. Report Centre Farm at C.7.a.

3. ACKNOWLEDGE.

From 3rd Cavalry Division
Place H.19.b.
Time 01.15.

(Sd) G.P.COSENS, Lt.Col.

Append 220

"A" Form
MESSAGES AND SIGNALS.

Army Form C. 2121
(In pads of 100.)

TO	6th Cav. Bde.	Cavalry Corps.
	7th Cav. Bde.	C.R.H.A.
	Candn. Cav. Bde.	

Sender's Number.	Day of Month.	In reply to Number.	
G.C.31.	9th		AAA

In continuation of 3rd Cav. Div. Order No.70, after 1st Bound AAA

2nd Bound. Should the situation then permit, the high ground N. and E. of LE CATEAU will then be occupied and preparations made for a further advance on VALENCIENNES AAA In consequence

(A) 7th Cav.Bde. will push forward reconnaissances to FOREST, AMERVAL, NEUVILLY.

(B) 6th Cav. Bde. will push forward and occupy high ground N. and E. of LE CATEAU pushing reconnaissances to BAZUEL and POMMEREUIL. The railway line S.E. of LE CATEAU is to be cut as soon as possible.

(C) Canadian Cav.Bde. will seize with one Regt. the high ground on spur K.31.a. & b. maintaining touch with the left of 7th Cav. Bde. remainder of Brigade coming into Divl. support.

/2

"A" Form
MESSAGES AND SIGNALS.

Army Form C. 2121 (In pads of 100.)

Sender's Number.	Day of Month.	In reply to Number.	
G.C.31.	9th		AAA

ACKNOWLEDGE.

Addressed 3 Bdes. and C.R.H.A., repeated Cavalry Corps.

From 3rd Cavalry Division.
Place C.7.a.
Time 07.10.

(Z) (Sd) G.P.COSENS, Lt.Col.

Appendix 21

"A" Form
MESSAGES AND SIGNALS.

Army Form C. 2121 (In pads of 100.)

TO		
6th Cav. Bde.	C.R.H.A.	
7th Cav. Bde.	Cavalry Corps.	
Can. Cav. Bde.	1st Cavalry Divn.	

Sender's Number.	Day of Month.	In reply to Number.	AAA
G.C.32.	9th		

Division is moving forward on a two Brigade frontage, 6th Cavalry Bde. on right, Canadian Cav. Bde. on left, 7th Cavalry Bde. in Divisional support AAA Objectives as already given in 3rd Cav. Div. Order No.70. AAA Addsd 3 Brigades and C.R.H.A. reptd Cav. Corps and 1st Cav. Div.

From: 3rd Cavalry Division.
Place: U.26.b.9.1.
Time: 09.20.

(Z)(Sd) G.P.COSENS, Lt.Col.

Appendix 22

"A" Form
MESSAGES AND SIGNALS.

Army Form C. 2121
(In pads of 100.)

No. of Message............

Prefix........Code........m.	Words	Charge.	This message is on a/c of:	Recd. at......m.
	Sent			Date...........
Office of Origin and Service Instructions	At........m.		........Service.	From..........
	To			
	By		(Signature of "Franking Officer")	By..........

TO — 6th Cavalry Brigade.

| Sender's Number. | Day of Month. | In reply to Number. | AAA |
| G.H.10. | 9th | | |

You must push on at once AAA Bosche transport is retreating through LE CATEAU and we must get forward to deny him the road running East through LE CATEAU.

I will support you closely with 7th Cavalry Bde

From: 3rd Cavalry Division.
Place: P.27.b.
Time: 16.00

(Z) (Sd.) S.G. HOWES, Major for G.O.C

Appendix 23

"A" Form
MESSAGES AND SIGNALS.

Army Form C. 2121 (In pads of 100.)

TO	7th Cavalry Brigade.	6th Cav. Bde. Can. Cav. Bde.

Sender's Number.	Day of Month.	In reply to Number.	
G.C.46.	9th		AAA

6th Cav. Bde. are held up line of trenches ST.SOUPLET to REUMONT AAA Move west of HONNECHY and MAUROIS in support of Canadian Cav. Bde. whose H.Q. were last reported at P.21.c.1.7. AAA Endeavour to push on in conjunction with Canadian Cav. Bde. to a position which will deny the roads going eastwards through LE CATEAU to the enemy AAA Addsd 7th Cavalry Bde., reptd. 6th and Canadian Cav. Bdes.

From 3rd Cavalry Divn.
Place P.27.b.
Time 16.55.

(Sd) G.P.COSENS, Lt.Col.

Appendix 24

"A" Form
MESSAGES AND SIGNALS.

Army Form C. 2121 (In pads of 100.)

TO:
6th Cav.Bde.	3rd Fd.Sqdn.	A.D.M.S.
7th Cav.Bde.	3rd Sig.Sqdn.	A.D.V.S.
~~Candn.Cav.Bde.~~	C.R.H.A.	
A.1 Echelon.	Camp Commdt.	S.A.A.Sect.D.A.C

Sender's Number: G.C.55
Day of Month: 9th
AAA

Units will be ready at 06.00 tomorrow morning further orders as soon as received.

From: 3rd Cavalry Divn.
Place: P.26.d.3.9.
Time: 20.45.

(Z) (Sd) C.KERR, Lt.Col.

SECRET.

3rd Cavalry Division Order No.71.

Reference 1/40,000 Sheet 57B.   October 10th, 1918.

1.   The successful advance of Fourth and Third Armies will be continued today.

2.   Objectives as follows:-

        XIII Corps   ...   LE CATEAU.
        V Corps   ...   directed on NEUVILLY.
        IV Corps   ...   directed on BRIASTRE.

3.   Task of Cavalry Corps is to continue to advance on objectives already laid down.

4.   In consequence 3rd Cavalry Division will move at 06.00 and cross R. SELLE between MONTAY and NEUVILLY (both inclusive). Its objective will be high ground FOREST K.12.c. & d. to AMERVAL K.4.b. both inclusive.
      It will send detachments early in direction of LE CATEAU to ascertain situation there.

  (b)   1st Cavalry Division will have its head at P.6.central by 07.00.

  (c)   4th Guards Brigade will have its head just short of REUMONT by 07.30.

  (d)   Household M.G. Brigade follow 4th Guards Brigade.

  (e)   17th Armoured Car Battn. and XVIII Corps Cyclists remain under 3rd Cavalry Division.

5.   In consequence, 7th Cavalry Brigade, plus 1 Field Troop and 3 Armoured Cars and "D" Battery 23rd Brigade A.F.A. attached, will carry out role allotted to 3rd Cavalry Division above and with its advanced detachments will pass through Canadian Cavalry Brigade whose line is approx. K.31.a. - K.19.cent. - RAMBOURLIEUX FME - K.13.a. at 06.00 hours.
      It will send reconnaissances at 06.30 between LE CATEAU - MONTAY - NEUVILLY.

  (b)   So soon as 7th Cavalry Brigade have passed through them, Canadian Cavalry Brigade will concentrate about TROISVILLES.

  (c)   6th Cavalry Brigade, with 1 Field Troop, will concentrate by 06.00 in valley P.5.c.

6.   XVIII Corps Cyclists will report to 3rd Cavalry Division H.Q. at X-roads P.4.b.5.0. so soon as relieved or passed through by advancing Infantry.

7.   17th Armoured Car Battalion less 3 Cars will report at X-roads P.4.b.5.0. by 06.00.

8.   A.1 Echelon and S.A.A.Section D.A.C. will be concentrated about P.14.d. just South of BERTRY by 07.30.

9.   Field Ambulances and Mobile Vet. Sections will remain divisionalized under A.D.M.S. and A.D.V.S. respectively.

10.   Divisional H.Q., 3rd Signal Squadron, 3rd Field Squadron less 2 Troops, will be concentrated at X-roads P.4.b.5.0. by 06.00 at which hour report centre will open there.

                                                                                          ....11.

"A" Form
MESSAGES AND SIGNALS.

Army Form C. 2121
(In pads of 100.)

Prefix......Code......m.	Words	Charge.	This message is on a/c of:	Recd. at......m.
Office of Origin and Service Instructions	Sent			Date...........
	At .... m.		..................Service.	From ....
	To			
	By		(Signature of "Franking Officer")	By..........

TO — All concerned.

Sender's Number.	Day of Month.	In reply to Number.	AAA
G.C.69.	10th		

(1) Brigades (less Batteries) and Units of Divisional Troops will move forthwith into bivouac areas about MONTIGNY.

(2) 6th Cav. Bde. and 1 Field Troop R.E. attached to Squares O.12.b. & d.

7th Cav. Bde. and 1 Field Troop R.E. attached to Squares P.13.b., P.14.a., P.8.c., P.7.d.

Canadian Cav. Bde. Squares O.5.d., O.11.b.

Village of MONTIGNY allotted to 6th Cav. Bde. N. and E. of BERTRY-LIGNY Road and to Canadian Cav. Bde. S. & W. of that road.

Div. H.Q., 3rd Sig.Sqdn. & 3rd Field Sqdn. (less 2 troops) O.12.d.

A.1 Echelon and S.A.A.Sect.D.A.C. will remain in present position P.14.d..

6th & 7th Cav.Fd.Ambces. will remain at BERTRY under orders of A.D.M.S.

From
Place
Time

The above may be forwarded as now corrected. (Z)

....
Censor.   Signature of Addressor or person authorised to telegraph in his name
* This line should be erased if not required.

Order No. 1625. Wt. W3253/ P 511 27/2 H. & K., Ltd. (E. 2634).

"A" Form
MESSAGES AND SIGNALS.

Army Form C. 2121 (In pads of 100.)

Sender's Number.	Day of Month.	In reply to Number.	AAA
G.C.69	10th		

Canadian Cav.Fd.Ambce. will rejoin Canadian Cav. Bde.

Mobile Vet.Sections will remain Divisionalized under A.D.V.S.

(3) Routes to bivouac area any across country where possible.

(4) Batteries R.H.A. and R.C.H.A.Bde. and "D" Battery 23rd A.F.A.Bde. will come under orders of C.R.H.A. for remainder of day and will rejoin Brigades at night. "D" Battery 23rd A.F.A.Bde. to Div.Troops area under orders of C.R.H.A.

(5) A.2 Echelon & Light Sect.Res.Park will move under orders of "Q" to O.18.b. & d.

(6) Heavy Sect. D.A.C. will remain in present area W. of MARETZ.

(7) Divisional Report Centre MONTIGNY Ch. until further orders from 15.00.

From	3rd Cavalry Division.
Place	P.4.d.central
Time	14.15.

(Z) (Sd) S.G.HOWES, Major.

"A" Form
MESSAGES AND SIGNALS.

Army Form C. 2121 (In pads of 100.)

TO: All concerned.

Sender's Number.	Day of Month.	In reply to Number.	
G.C.72	10th		AAA

Brigades and Divisional Troops will be watered saddled up and ready to move by 08.30 tomorrow Octo. 11th AAA Addressed all concerned.

From 3rd Cavalry Division.
Place O.11.d.5.8.
Time 19.15.

(Sd) S.G. HOWES, Major, G.S.

Appendix 28
SECRET.

3rd Cavalry Division Order No.72.   Copy No........

Reference Map
1/40,000 Sheet 57B.   11th October, 1918.

1. Following moves will take place today, October 11th.

   (a) 6th Cavalry Brigade will move to ELINCOURT starting at 13.30.
   (b) A.1 Echelons will rejoin Brigades and Units of Divisional Troops at 16.00.
   (c) A.2 Echelons will rejoin Brigades and Units of Divisional Troops at 16.00.
   (d) Light Sections Cavalry Field Ambulances will rejoin Brigades at 15.00 under orders of A.D.M.S.
   (e) S.A.A. Section D.A.C. will rejoin D.A.C. at 16.00 at O.12.b.5.0.
   (f) Field Troops R.E. now attached to 6th and 7th Cavalry Brigades will rejoin 3rd Field Squadron at O.11.d. on CLARY-CAUDRY Road at 16.00.
   (g) Divisional H.Q., H.Q. R.H.A., H.Q. A.S.C., & 3rd Signal Squadron will move this afternoon to outskirts of BERTRY. Exact location will be notified later.

2. Roads to be avoided during move as much as possible, and mounted troops to move on a broad front.

3. Location 7th Cavalry Bde. H.Q. Billet No.5, BERTRY, P.14.b.3.9.
   Location Canadian Cavalry Bde. H.Q. near big Church, MONTIGNY, O.12.a.3.7.

4. Brigades and Units of Divisional Troops will send guides to A.1 Echelon at P.14.d. and to A.2 Echelon at O.18.b.4.2. by 14.00 to guide their echelons to units.

5. Mobile Veterinary Sections will remain divisionalized under orders of A.D.V.S. until further notice.

6. Divisional Report Centre will remain at O.11.d.5.3. for the present and will reopen at BERTRY at an hour to be notified later.

7. ACKNOWLEDGE.

                                                Major,
Issued at 12.15 hours.   G.S., 3rd Cavalry Division.

Copies to:-
No.1 6th Cav. Bde.   12   A.P.M.
   2 7th Cav. Bde.   13   Camp Commdt.
   3 Candn. Cav. Bde.   14-15   O.C. A.S.C.
   4 3rd Sig. Sqdn.   16   O.C. Div.A.1 Echelon.
   5 3rd Fd. Sqdn.   17   O.C. Div.A.2 Echelon.
   6 C.R.H.A.   18   Cavalry Corps.
   7 D.A.C.   19   1st Cavalry Division.
   8 S.A.A. Section D.A.C.
   9 "Q"
  10 A.D.M.S.
  11 A.D.V.S.

"A" Form
MESSAGES AND SIGNALS.

Army Form C. 2121
(In pads of 100.)

TO: All concerned.

Sender's Number: G.C.83
Day of Month: 11th

AAA

Brigades and Units of Divisional Troops are at 3½ hours notice from receipt of orders at Brigade and Unit H.Q. AAA Addressed all concerned.

From: 3rd Cavalry Division
Place: O.11.d.5.8.
Time: 12.30.

(Z) (Sd) G.P.COSENS, Lt.Col.

Appendix 20

S E C R E T.

3rd Cavalry Division Order No. 73.   Copy No........

Reference Map 1/100,000 VALENCIENNES 12.   13th Oct., 1918.

1. 3rd Cavalry Division will move today, October 13th, and tomorrow, October 14th, to an area about ETRICOURT - YTRES - HENNOIS WOOD, staging for night 13/14th on the CANAL DE ST. QUENTIN between BANTOUZELLE and HONNECOURT.

2. Divisional Headquarters, H.Q., R.H.A., H.Q. A.S.C. and 3rd Signal Squadron will march through today, October 13th, to HENNOIS WOOD.

3. 6th Cavalry Brigade to start at 07.00.
   Route - MALINCOURT - VILLERS OUTREAUX.

   Divisional Headquarters, H.Q. R.H.A., H.Q. A.S.C. and 3rd Signal Squadron to start at 07.45.
   Route - MALINCOURT - VILLERS OUTREAUX - HONNECOURT - FINS.
   Destination - HENNOIS WOOD, just South of MANANCOURT.

   3rd Field Squadron - Starting Point SELVIGNY. Time - 08.30.
   Route MALINCOURT - VILLERS OUTREAUX (to march to S.P. via CLARY).

   Canadian Cavalry Brigade - Starting Point SELVIGNY. Time 09.00.
   Route as for 3rd Field Squadron.

   7th Cavalry Brigade - Starting Point SELVIGNY. Time 10.30.
   Route as for 3rd Field Squadron.

   D.A.C. - Starting Point SELVIGNY. Time 12.00.
   Route as for 3rd Field Squadron.

   Light Section, 3rd Cavalry Reserve Park. Starting Point SELVIGNY. Route - as for 3rd Field Squadron.

4. Staff Captains, Adjutant R.H.A., Adjutant A.S.C. will meet Divisional Staff Officer at 09.30 at road junction at Farm 1 mile S.E. of Z of BANTOUZELLE (Reference Map 1/40,000 57B, S.10.b.1.8.), to be allotted areas.

5. Mounted troops will march off roads wherever posible. Distances as laid down in S.S. 724 will be maintained when troops and vehicles are on the road.

6. Mobile Veterinary Sections will move under the orders of A.D.V.S. who will notify Brigades direct when they will rejoin Brigades.
   Light Sections Cavalry Field Ambulances accompany Brigades.

7. Divisional Report Centre will close at   ELINCOURT at 12.00 and reopen at HENNOIS WOOD at same hour.

7. ACKNOWLEDGE.

                                              Major,
Issued at 00.30.   G.S., 3rd Cavalry Division.

Distribution:-
6th C. B.	C.R.H.A.	A.P.M.	Cav. Corps.
7th C. B.	D.A.C.	Camp Commdt.	1st Cav. Div.
Can.C. B.	"Q"	O.C. A.S.C.	
3rd Sig.Sqdn.	A.D.M.S.	Light Sec. 3rd Cav.Res.Pk.	
3rd Fd. Sqdn.	A.D.V.S.	Div. "B" Echelon.	

Appendix 31

SECRET.
Copy No......

3rd Cavalry Division Order No. 54.

Reference Map 1/40,000
Sheet 57 C.

13th October, 1918.

1. The march of the 3rd Cavalry Division will be continued tomorrow, October 14th, to the YTRES - ETRICOURT Area in accordance with March Table overleaf.

2. **Following Restrictions:-**

   (a) Transport only will march through GOUZEAUCOURT.

   (b) All mounted troops will move round GOUZEAUCOURT across country.

   (c) The Division will use the road through V.12.b. & a. through FINS, and not the road through the middle of the village, V.12.d. and c.

   (d) The Division will be West of GOUZEAUCOURT by 16.00.

   (e) Mounted troops will march across country wherever possible.

3. Distances as laid down in S.S.724 will be maintained on the road.

4. Divisional Report Centre remains at DESSOIS WOOD, U.24.

5. Acknowledge.

Major,
G.S., 3rd Cavalry Division.

Issued at 18.00.

Copies to:-

No.		No.	
1	6th Cavalry Bde.	13-14	O.C.A.S.C.
2	7th Cavalry Bde.	15	Light Section, 3rd Cav. Reserve Park.
3	Canadian Cav. Bde.		
4	3rd Signal Sqdn.	16	Heavy Section, 3rd Cav. Reserve Park.
5	3rd Field Sqdn.		
6	C.R.H.A.	17	Aux. H.T. Coy.
7	D.A.C.	18	O.C. Div. "B" Echelon.
8	"Q"	19	Cavalry Corps.
9	A.D.M.S.		
10	A.D.V.S.		
11	A.P.M.		
12	Camp Commandant.		

March Table issued with 3rd Cavalry Division Order No.64.

Serial No.	Date. Oct.	Unit.	Starting Point.	Time to pass S.P.	Route.	Destination.	Remarks.
1.	14th	6th Cav. Bde.	GOMELIEU.	08.00	GOUZEAUCOURT - FINS - EQUANCOURT	Part of HENNOIS WOOD - MANANCOURT - ETRICOURT & as far North as Station in P.32.d.	Details of billets from D.A.& Q.M.G. 3rd Cavalry Divn.
2.	14th	7th Cav. Bde.	VILLERS GUISLAIN.	09.15	As for Serial No.1.	BERTINCOURT - RUYAULCOURT - NEUVILLE BOURJONVAL YTRES.	Details of billets from Area Commdt., YTRES.
3.	14th	Canadian Cav. Brigade.	GOMELIEU.	10.30.	do. do.	YTRES - BUS.	do. do.
4.	14th	3rd Field Sqdn.	As for Serial No. 2.	11.45	do. do.	HENNOIS WOOD U.24.	Billets from D.A.& Q.M.G., 3rd Cavalry Divn.
5.	14th	T.A.C.	do.	12.00	do. do.	LECHELLE.	
6.	14th	Light Soctn., 3rd Cav. Res. Park.	do.	13.15.	do. do.	LE MESNIL - EN - ARROUAISE.	A.M.T. Coy. & Heavy Section 3rd Cav.Res.Park will also be accommodated in this area.

Appendix 32

SECRET.

3rd Cavalry Division Order No. 75.   Copy No.......

Reference Maps 1/100,000,
LENS & VALENCIENNES.   14th October, 1918.

1.   "B" Echelon, Heavy Section 3rd Cavalry Reserve Park, and Auxiliary H.T. Company will move today as soon as possible, after receipt of these orders, to rejoin the Division in the YTRES-ETRICOURT Area.
       No restrictions as to roads.

2.   On arrival, "B" Echelon will rejoin Brigades and Units of Divisional Troops in areas as shown in 3rd Cavalry Division Order No. 74.

3.   Heavy Section Reserve Park and Auxiliary H.T. Company to LE MESNIL-EN-ARROUAISE.

4.   Distances as laid down in S.S.734 will be maintained on the road.

5.   ACKNOWLEDGE.

                                        C. Rowcroft
                                            for
                                        Lieut.Colonel,
Issued at 06.00.   G.S., 3rd Cavalry Division.

Copies to:-
    No.1 6th Cavalry Brigade.
      2   7th Cavalry Brigade.
      3   Canadian Cavalry Brigade.
      4   3rd Signal Squadron.
      5   3rd Field Squadron.
      6   C.R.H.A.
      7   "Q".
      8   A.P.M.
      9   Camp Commandant.
   10-11 O.C. A.S.C.
     12   Light Section, 3rd Cav.Res.Park.
     13   Heavy Section, 3rd Cav.Res.Park.
     14   Aux. H.T. Company.
     15   O.C. Divisionalized "B" Echelon.
     16   Cavalry Corps.

Confidential

War Diary
of
General Staff,
3rd Cavalry Division
Intelligence Summaries
November, 1918.

Appendix 1

SECRET.
Copy No. 22

3rd Cavalry Division Order No. 76.

Reference Maps VALENCIENNES and LENS 1/100,000.   6th November, 1918.

1. 3rd Cavalry Division will move today, November 6th, to a Staging Area SAUCHY - LESTREE - MARQUION - SAINS-lez-MARQUION - INCHY-en-ARTOIS - BUISSY - BARALLE - SAUCHY-CAUCHY as follows.

   (a) 7th Cavalry Brigade to SAUCHY-CAUCHY and SAUCHY-LESTREE.
       Route: HERMIES - MOEUVRES - X roads M of MARQUION.
       To be North of HERMIES by 10.30.
       7th Cavalry Brigade will accommodate XVIII Corps Cyclists, strength 300, in their area.

   (b) 6th Cavalry Brigade to MARQUION and SAINS-lez-MARQUION.
       Starting Point METZ-en-COUTURE 10.15.
       Route TRESCAULT - HAVRINCOURT - R of MOEUVRES.

   (c) Canadian Cavalry Brigade to BUISSY and BARALLE.
       Starting Point HERMIES 10.30.
       Route MOEUVRES - INCHY.

   (d) Divisional Ammunition Column to INCHY-en-ARTOIS.
       Starting Point HERMIES 12.00.
       Route MOEUVRES.

   (e) 3rd Signal Squadron, Divisional H.Q. Details, H.Q. 4th Bde. R.H.A. H.Q., A.S.C. to INCHY-en-ARTOIS.
       Starting Point METZ-en-COUTURE 11.45.
       Route HAVRINCOURT - MOEUVRES, in order of march as stated.

   (f) 3rd Field Squadron to INCHY-en-ARTOIS.
       Starting Point METZ. Time 12.15.
       Route as for Divisional H.Q. Details.

   (g) Aux. H.T. Coy. to INCHY-en-ARTOIS.
       Starting Point BERTINCOURT 11.15.
       Route HERMIES - MOEUVRES.

   (h) 3rd Cav. Res. Park to INCHY-en-ARTOIS.
       Starting Point 11.30.
       Route as for Aux. H.T. Coy.

2. "A" and "B" Echelons will accompany Brigades and Units of Divisional Troops.

3. Distances as laid down in S.S.724.

4. Representatives from each Unit of Divisional Troops billeted in INCHY-en-ARTOIS will meet a Divisional Staff Officer at road junction in centre of INCHY-en-ARTOIS at 11.00 to be allotted areas.

5. Divisional Report Centre will remain at HENNOIS WOOD.

6. Acknowledge.

Issued at 02.30.

                                              Major,
                          G.S., 3rd Cavalry Division.

Addressed List "A".

To all Recipients of 3rd Cavalry Division Order No.77.
===

Reference para. 1, Divisional area is allotted as follows:-

6th Cavalry Brigade and XVIII Corps Cyclists Battalion - ESQUERCHIN.

7th Cavalry Brigade - LAUWIN and PLANQUET.

Canadian Cavalry Brigade - CUINCHY.

Divisional H.Q.Details, H.Q. A.S.C.Details, 3rd Signal Squadron Details, H.Q. R.H.A. - W. suburbs of DOUAI, West of Canal.

D.A.C. and 3rd Field Squadron R.E. - WAGNONVILLE. Area to be allotted by O.C. D.A.C.

3rd Cav.Res.Park and Aux. H.T.Coy. - DOUAI Prison. Area to be allotted by O.C. Reserve Park.

6th November, 1918.

Major,
G.S., 3rd Cavalry Division.

Appendix 2

SECRET.

3rd Cavalry Division Order No. 77.   Copy No.........

Reference Map 1/100,000 VALENCIENNES & TOURNAI. 6th November, 1918.

1. 3rd Cavalry Division will continue the march tomorrow, November 7th, to a Divisional Staging Area LAUWIN - CUINCY - PRISON - ESQUERCHIN.
    Details and allotment of area will be notified later.

2. "B" Echelons of Brigades and Divisional Troops and Heavy Sections C.F.As. will be divisionalized at western exit of EPINOY at 11.00, and march divisionalized under Captain JENKINS, 7th Dragoon Guards, as per March Table, but will rejoin Brigades and Divisional Troops on arrival in area West of DOUAI.

3. Distances as laid down in S.S.724 will be maintained.

4. A Divisional Staff Officer will meet Brigades and units of Divisional Troops between CANTIN and BUGNICOURT to point out water points on CANAL de la SENSEE.

5. All troops and transport of the Division will be North of BUGNICOURT by 13.00 hours.

6. Rate of march for Brigades 4 miles per hour.

7. Divisional Report Centre will close at HENNOIS WOOD at 13.00 hours and reopen temporarily at CYSOING, 7 miles S.E. of LILLE, at same hour.

8. ACKNOWLEDGE.

Issued at 17.30.

Major,
G.S., 3rd Cavalry Division.

Copies to List "A", plus O.C. Divisionalized "B" Echelon.

March Table issued with 3rd Cavalry Division Order No.77.

Serial No.	Date Nov.	Unit.	Starting Point.	Time to pass S.P.	Route.	Destination.	Remarks.
1.	7th	7th Cavalry Bde.	Any.	—	RUMANCOURT - ECOURT ST.QUENTIN - PALLUEL - ARLEUX DOUAI.	Divisional area just West of DOUAI.	To be North of BUGNICOURT by 09.00.
2.	7th	6th Cavalry Bde.	Any.	—	EPINOY - AUBENCHEUL AU BAC - BUGNICOURT - DOUAI.	ditto.	Head of column to enter BUGNICOURT at 09.00.
3.	7th	Canadian Cav.Bde.	ECOURT ST. QUENTIN, S. exit.	08.00.	As for Serial No. 1.	ditto.	To give precedence to 6th Cavalry Bde. at CANTIN.
4.	7th	3rd Field Sqdn.	X roads M of MARQUION.	08.45.	As for Serial No. 2.	ditto.	To give precedence to Canadian Cav.Bde. between BUGNICOURT & CANTIN.
5.	7th	3rd Signal Sqdn. Divl.H.Q.Details H.Q., R.H.A. H.Q., A.S.C.	As for Serial No. 4.	09.00.	As for Serial No. 2.	ditto.	
6.	7th	D.A.C.	ditto.	09.15.	ditto.	ditto.	
7.	7th	Aux. M.T.Coy.	ditto.	09.30.	ditto.	ditto.	
8.	7th	3rd Cav. Reserve Park.	ditto.	09.40.	ditto.	ditto.	
9.	7th	Divl.B.Echelon & Heavy Sects. C.F.A.S.	EPINOY.	11.00.	ditto.	ditto.	

Appendix 5
SECRET

List "A".
XVIII Corps Cyclists.
1st Cavalry Division.

G.575.
8.11.18.

Reference Maps 1/100,000, VALENCIENNES and TOURNAI.

1. 3rd Cavalry Division and XVIII Corps Cyclists will continue march tomorrow, November 8th, as follows:-

2. "A" & "B" Echelons accompany Brigades, etc.

3. Details, 3rd Signal Squadron, Divisional H.Q., H.Q., R.H.A., and H.Q. A.S.C. to SAINGHIN.
   Starting Point fork roads 400 yards North of D of DOUAI.
   Time - 06.30.
   Route - RACHE - BERSEE - MOLPAS.

4. Canadian Cavalry Brigade to area ENNETIERES - AVELIN - MARTINSART - SECLIN. (Billets from Cavalry Corps "Q" for SECLIN).
   Starting Point as for 3rd Signal Squadron.
   Time - 07.00.
   Route - as for 3rd Signal Squadron.

5. 6th Cavalry Brigade to area FRETIN - PERONNE - LOUVIL.
   Starting Point as for 3rd Signal Squadron.
   Time - 08.30.
   Route - RACHE - BERSEE - MOLPAS - TEMPLEUVE.

6. 3rd Field Squadron to ATTICHES.
   Starting Point AUBY.
   Time - 08.00.
   Route - LE FOREST - MONCHEAUX - THUMERIES.

7. D.A.C. to PETIT ATTICHES
   Starting Point and Route as for 3rd Field Squadron.
   Time - 08.15.

8. Aux. H.T. Company to WATTIESSART.
   Starting Point and Route as for 3rd Field Squadron.
   Time - 08.30.

9. 3rd Cavalry Reserve Park to PHALEMPIN (all North of Church).
   Starting Point and Route as for 3rd Field Squadron.
   Time 08.45.

10. 7th Cavalry Brigade to area LANEUVILLE - WAHAGNIES - OSTRICOURT.
    Starting Point - AUBY.
    Time 09.45.
    Route - LE FOREST.

11. XVIII Corps Cyclists to PONT-A-MARCQ.
    Starting Point - as for 3rd Field Squadron.
    Time - 10.00.
    Route - main DOUAI-LILLE Road.

12. All troops marching on main DOUAI-LILLE Road to be North of DOUAI by 10.00 and North of MOLPAS by 13.00. Troops are to march either on the pave or right clear of the road, and not the mud fringe of pave.

13. Distances as laid down in S.S.724.

14. Divisional Report Centre is located at SAINGHIN.

15. ACKNOWLEDGE.

Issued at 01.00.
8th Nov..1918.

(Sd) S.G.HOWES, Major,
G.S., 3rd Cavalry Division.

Appendix 4

SECRET.

3rd Cavalry Division Order No. 78.   Copy No...92...

Reference Map 1/100,000 TOURNAI.   8th November, 1918.

1. 7th Cavalry Brigade (with 1 Section of Field Troop R.E. and detachment of Light Section, 3rd Cavalry Reserve Park, attached), but less "K" Battery R.H.A. will move to Second Army area tomorrow, 9th inst.
March to commence at 08.30 hours.
Route in Fifth Army area as follows:-
AVELIN - LESQUIN - RONCHIN - LEZENNES - HELLEMMES - LA MADELINE.
Orders for march and instructions etc. in Second Army area are as given in Second Army G.446 dated 8th instant attached.(Reference para.1, for "1 Cavalry Brigade" read "7th Cavalry Brigade").
Routes are shewn on Map "A" and crossings on Map "B" (maps attached for 7th Cavalry Brigade only).

2. Orders for one Section Field Troop, and for detachment of Light Section Reserve Park, to join 7th Cavalry Brigade on the march will be issued direct by 7th Cavalry Brigade/°3rd Field Squadron and 3rd Cavalry Reserve Park.
(3rd Field Squadron is billeted at ATTICHES, 3rd Cavalry Reserve Park at PHALEMPIN).

3. "K" Battery R.H.A. will be attached to and accommodated by 6th Cavalry Brigade from 9th instant inclusive, and will march at 10.00 hours November 9th, to Northern outskirts of SAINGHIN (billets from 3rd Cavalry Division "Q").
Any route.

4. ACKNOWLEDGE.

                                       [signature]. Major,
                                       G.S., 3rd Cavalry Division.

Issued at 19.15.

Distribution - List "A".

Appendix 4

SECRET.
                                                                          Second Army.
                                                                          G.446.
                                                                      8th Nov., 1918.

XIX Corps.
X Corps.
XV Corps.
----

1.   1 Cavalry Brigade (British) has been placed at the disposal of Second Army and will march into the Army area on 9th instant.

2.   1 Regiment is posted to each of the X and XIX Corps and will be accommodated by Corps at STE. ANNE (N.19.) and CUERNE respectively.

    Details of accommodation will be obtained

        For STE ANNE   36th Division "Q".
        For CUERNE   XIX Corps "Q".

3.   The Brigade less the above 2 Regiments will be held in Army reserve, accommodated in the western outskirts of TURCOING, F.3. and 9, and administered by XV Corps.

    Details of accommodation will be obtained from the Commandant, TURCOING (Town Hall, TURCOING).

4.   Routes to billeting areas are shewn on attached map marked "A".

5.   The attached map marked "B" shews bridges over the LYS and the COURTRAI - L'ESCAUT and ROUBAIX - L'ESCAUT Canals.

6.   Headquarters of the above mentioned units are as follows:-

        XIX Corps   ...   POTTELBERG (S. of COURTRAI).
        X Corps   ...   LE TRIER DES PRETRES (N.W. of
                                            NEUVILLE AU FERRAIN).
        XV Corps   ...   MOUVAUX F.15.c.
        36th Division..   MOUSCRON (The Mairie).

7.   Acknowledge.

                                            (Sd) E.R.MANTEN, Captain, G.S
                                                for M.G. G.S., Second Army

Copies to:-
    Adv. G.H.Q.
    Fifth Army (3) with maps.
    II Corps.
    "Q".
    C.E.
    D.P.M.
    Signals.

Appendix 5

3rd Cavalry Division Order No. 79.   SECRET.

Reference Map 1/100,000 TOURNAI.   Copy No........

10th November, 1918.

1.   3rd Cavalry Division (less 7th Cavalry Brigade and "B" Echelons of 6th and Canadian Cavalry Brigades and Divisional Troops, Heavy Sections C.F.As., Heavy Section D.A.C., Heavy Section Reserve Park, and Aux. H.T. Company) will move today to LA GLANERIE - LA VERTE RUE - COBRIEUX - BACHY as follows:-

   6th Cavalry Brigade and "K" Battery R.H.A. to BACHY and both sides of main CYSOING - MOUCHIN Road from BACHY to LA CRINQUET Station, to start at 08.00.
   Route - CYSOING.

   Canadian Cavalry Brigade to COBRIEUX and LA POSTERIE, to start at 09.00.
   Route - WACHEMY - GENECH.

   3rd Field Squadron (less detachments) to LA VERTE RUE, to start at 09.00.
   Route - PONT A MARCQ - CAPPELLE - OUVIGNIES.

   S.A.A. Section D.A.C. to start at 09.30.
   Route and destination as for 3rd Field Squadron.

   Light Section Reserve Park to start at 10.00.
   Route and destination as for 3rd Field Squadron.

   Divisional H.Q. plus 1 Field Troop R.E., 3rd Signal Squadron, H.Q. R.H.A., H.Q. A.S.C. to LA GLANERIE, to start at 10.00.
   Route - CYSOING.

2.   Billeting representatives from 3rd Field Squadron, 3rd Cavalry Reserve Park, and S.A.A. Section D.A.C. to meet Divisional Staff Officer at the road junction ½ mile North of T of LA VERTE RUE at 10.00.

3.   "B" Echelons of 6th and Canadian Cavalry Brigades and units of Divisional Troops, and Heavy Sections C.F.As. will be concentrated at MARTINSART under an Officer to be detailed by 6th Cavalry Brigade - to march from present areas at 12.00.

4.   Heavy Section D.A.C., Heavy Section Reserve Park, and Aux. H.T. Coy. remain in present areas.

5.   Distances as laid down in S.S.724.

6.   Divisional Report Centre will close at SAINGHIN at 12.00 and reopen at LA GLANERIE at same hour.

7.   ACKNOWLEDGE.

                                            J. Howis   Major,
                                            G.S., 3rd Cavalry Division.

Issued at 05.15.

Addressed List "A".

Appendix 6

SECRET.

3rd Cavalry Division Order No.80.   Copy No........

Reference 1/100,000, (TOURNAI.
)VALENCIENNES.
(BRUSSELS.   11th Nov., 1918.

1. First Army report that Cavalry have reached western outskirts of GHEIN. Aeroplane reports that Cavalry are in the BOIS DE BEAUDOIR approaching the railway. I Corps report that they hold NEUF MAISON and that Cavalry and Cyclists are in CHIEVRES. Our troops were reported just West of ATH at 14.35 hours.

2. The Cavalry Corps (less 7th Cavalry Brigade and Household M.G. Battalions) will move today, 11th, with objective the line SOIGNIES - ENGHIEN.

3. The first bound will be the line MASNUY-STE-PIERRE - FROIDMONT - THORICOURT - SILLY, but Divisions will not wait for each other on this line, but will push forward to their final objectives.
Dividing line between Divisions ELLIGNIES-STE-ANNE - CHIEVRES - THORICOURT - STEENKERQUE, all inclusive to 1st Cavalry Division.

4. (a) 1st Cavalry Division, less 9th Cavalry Brigade, will move at 08.00 hours and pick up the 1st Cavalry Brigade which has already been ordered by the I Corps to seize the line MASNUY-STE-PIERRE - FROIDMONT - THORICOURT today this morning.
1st Cavalry Division will move by any road within its area.

(b) 9th Cavalry Brigade will be assembled at ATH this morning and come into Corps Reserve.

(c) 3rd Cavalry Division will move at 08.00 hours. The leading Cavalry Brigade and Batteries and A.1 Echelon will use the main TOURNAI - ATH road, and the head of leading Brigade will pass Y road ½ mile North of the 2nd R in BARRY at 08.15. All other troops will move South of that road.

5. In consequence:-

(a) 6th Cavalry Brigade, plus "K" Battery R.H.A. will act as advanced guard to the Division, and will seize objective as laid down in para. 2 above.
First bound as in para. 3 above.
Dividing line between Divisions as in para. 3 above.

(b) Canadian Cavalry Brigade will detail one Squadron Regiment to act as left flank guard to the Division, general line of advance South of and parallel to TOURNAI - LEUZE - ATH - ENGHIEN Road.

(c) Remainder of Division in order of march as under will move along general line VEZON - PONENCHE - WILLAUPUIS - TOURPES - BLICQUY - ORMEIGNIES - MAFFLE - GIBECQ - SILLY.

Escort troop as advanced guard.
Headquarters, 3rd Cavalry Division.
3rd Signal Squadron.
Canadian Cavalry Brigade (less 1 Squadron Regiment).
3rd Field Squadron R.E. (less 2 troops).
S.A.A. Section D.A.C.

Starting point X Roads just N.W. of V of VEZON at 08.45.

6. 3rd Field Squadron will detail one Troop to report to 6th and Canadian Cavalry Brigades forthwith.

7. One Flight No. 6 Squadron R.A.F. will work with 3rd Cavalry Division and carry out reconnaissances as under:-

-2-

    i. Report position of our Infantry and enemy troops North of LEUZE - ATH - ENGHIEN Road.

    ii. Report on the advance of our own troops.

    iii. Report whether ENGHIEN is held by the enemy.

8.   A.1 Echelons will be divisionalized at 09.30 at road junction ½ mile N. of 2nd R in BARRY, and will come under the orders of Lieut. MOTT, 3rd D.Gs. They will move forward from there to X Roads ¼ mile South of railway station at CHAPELLE-A-WATTINES, park clear of the road and await orders.

    Divisionalized A.2 Echelon and Light Section Reserve Park will move under the orders of A.A. & Q.M.G.

9.   Cavalry Field Ambulances and Mobile Veterinary Sections will be divisionalized by and come under the orders of A.D.M.S. and A.D.V.S. respectively.

10.   Divisional Report Centre will be at head of main body, moving as in para. 5 (c) above.

11.   ACKNOWLEDGE.

Issued at 06.00.

                                Lieut.Colonel,
                         G.S., 3rd Cavalry Division.

Distribution - List "B", less 7th Cav. Bde, D.M.G.O., and plus Liaisson Officer, 6th Sqdn.R.A.F., 1st Cav. Div.,

"A" Form
MESSAGES AND SIGNALS.

Army Form C. 2121
(In pads of 100.)

This message is on a/c of: Appendix

Date 8

TO: 1st Cavalry Div.
3rd Cavalry Div.

Sender's Number.	Day of Month.	In reply to Number.	AAA
G608	11th		

Armistice commenced 11.00 hours today AAA Divisions will withdraw to last night's area on receipt these orders AAA Main ATH BURNAI Road to be kept clear AAA Completion of withdrawal to be reported AAA 3rd Cav. Div. to inform 8th Hussars AAA Acknowledge by wireless

From: Cavalry Corps

Appendix 9

3RD. CAVALRY DIVISION ORDER NO. 81.   SECRET.

Copy No........

Reference Map 1/100,000.   12th. November, 1918.

1. Following redistribution of billeting Areas will take place as UNDER:-

     6th. Cavalry Brigade to BERTINCROIX - WARLDFOSSE - LIGNELLE - PONEMCHE - WILLAUPUIS - BAUGNIES - BRIFFOEIL - WASMES.

     Canadian Cavalry Brigade to FONTENOY - BOURGEON - BOUCHEGNETTE - MAUBRAY - MORLIES - PERONNES - VEZONCHAEUX - LE LARGE - ROSOIR - CREVECOEUR.

     3rd. Field Squadron R.E., S.A.A.Section D.A.C., Light Section Reserve Park to VEZON (billets from O.C. 3rd. Cavalry Division Reserve Park now located at VEZON).
     Troops of 1st. Corps in situ will not be moved.

2. There are no Area Commandants.

3. 6th. and Canadian Cavalry Brigades, 3rd. Field Squadron R.E., S.A.A.Section D.A.C. will move to above Areas today November, 12th.
     Moves to be completed by 1600 hours. No restrictions as to roads, but troops of Canadian Cavalry Brigade now billeted in BARRY will give precedence to 6th. Cavalry Brigade on the march.

4. Distances as laid down in S.S. 742.

5. Divisional Headquarters remains at ANTOING.

6. Acknowledge by bearer.

                                        S.G.Howis. Major,

12th. November, 1918.   G.S., 3rd. Cavalry Division.

Issued at 08.15

Addressed List "A" less D.A.C., plus S.A.A. Section D.A.C.

Appendix 10

SECRET.

INSTRUCTIONS No. 1.

ADVANCE OF CAVALRY CORPS TO GERMAN FRONTIER AFTER ARMISTICE
OF NOVEMBER 11th, 1918.

1. In accordance with the terms of the Armistice, the occupied portions of FRANCE, BELGIUM and LUXEMBURG are to be evacuated by the enemy by the 26th of November.

2. The Allied Forces will commence to advance on the 17th instant.

3. The advancing British Forces will be organized in two Armies, the Fourth Army on the right, and the Second on the left.

4. The Cavalry Corps (less 2nd Cavalry Division) will lead and cover the advance of the Second Army, and will come under orders of that Army. The 2nd Cavalry Division will be under the orders of the Fourth Army.
Until further orders the term Cavalry Corps will be read to mean the Cavalry Corps less 2nd Cavalry Division.

5. Reference Map attached (issued only to Cavalry Brigades and A.A. & Q.M.G.).

(a) Troops will cross our present front line on the 17th instant and will reach Line No.1 on the 18th instant. A halt of 48 hours will be made on this line.

(b) Troops will cross Line No.1 on the 21st instant, and reach Line No.2 on the 24th instant. Infantry will take four marches. It is probable that the Cavalry will cover it in three making a 24 hours halt en route.

(c) The advance from Line No.2 will take place on November 27th, and Line No.3 will be reached on December 2nd. (Note. The date of this advance will depend on the progress made with the Railways).

6. The enemy is to be clear of each of the three Zones mentioned above on the day preceding the commencement of our march into that Zone. Any enemy encountered on the march will therefore be made prisoner.
The following received from G.H.Q. is published for information:-
It has been brought to notice that in certain cases the Commanders of German Armies have requested the Commanders of Allied Armies facing them to enter into negotiations regarding the handing over of prisoners-of-war and war material. On no account will any communication be held with the Germans except under instructions issued by G.H.Q.

7. The Lines Nos. 1, 2 and 3 will each in turn form a frontier, and no troops are to pass these lines until orders to that effect are received.

8. The Cavalry Corps will advance on a two Division front, 1st Cavalry Division on the right, 3rd Cavalry Division on the left. Each Division will have two Brigades with their Batteries R.H.A. in the front line.

9. In consequence, the 3rd Cavalry Division will move forward/on a on Nov. 17th Two Brigade frontage, 6th Cavalry Brigade on right, 7th Cavalry Brigade on left, in accordance with 3rd Cavalry Division Order No. 82 issued herewith.
Dividing line between Brigades LESSINES - BIEVENE (both inclusive to 7th Cavalry Brigade) - point 2 miles N. of ENGHIEN on the ENGHIEN - DEUX WINDAKE Road.

.....Brigades.

- 2 -

Brigades will advance on a Two Regiment frontage, and all military precautions against surprise will be taken.

10. (a) Owing to the extensive front, it will not be possible to cover the whole of it with a continuous chain of outposts at night. Security will be obtained by Brigade Groups finding their own protection. This must be considered in selecting and allotting billets, as advanced Troops and Squadrons should also obtain cover.

(b) Each Brigade will therefore be responsible for its own outposts by day and night and will arrange to keep touch with the outposts of the Brigade on each flank.
A Brigade Outpost Officer will be detailed in each case.

(c) All main roads through Brigade areas must be blocked.

(d) 7th Cavalry Brigade will arrange to block roads leading from VOORDE to SCHENDELBEKE and OPHASSELT to GRAMMONT, and will be responsible for the protection of that flank of the advance.

(e) An inlying picket will be detailed by each Brigade and also such examining posts as may be necessary.

11. Civilians will be allowed to pass from east to west along roads occupied by our advanced squadrons, but not from west to east.

12. (a) Intelligence Officers of Divisions and Brigades will closely question civilians coming west as to how the Germans are carrying out the terms of the Armistice, especially as regards the retirement of their troops across Lines Nos. 1, 2 and 3, in accordance with the dates agreed upon.

(b) Intelligence Officers on arrival in billets will closely question inhabitants as to the presence of any Germans in the area. Should any be reported, they will be searched for and if found will be made prisoner and sent to Divisional H.Q. under escort.

13. One Field Troop R.E. is attached to each of the leading Brigades (6th and 7th).

14. Billeting parties will not be sent forward until the protective troops are east of the particular area allotted.

15. No cable will be laid during the advance. Wireless and Despatch Riders will be the means of communication. Messages may be sent over the wireless in clear, but code names will be used.

16. In order to assist the Infantry which will be following, reports on the roads used by the Cavalry must reach Divisional H.Q. by 15.00 hours on each day that an advance takes place. Obstructions only should be reported. Thus "Road from A to B destroyed at - " or "Bridge blown up at - " or "Road A to B impassable for troops and transport". These reports will be sent over the wireless in clear.

17. Completion of march and position of each Unit will be sent daily to Divisional H.Q. by Special D.R. immediately the march is completed.

18. Though the march forward will be conducted with all military precautions against surprise, every effort should be made to impress the inhabitants by the smartness and soldierly bearing of the troops.

......Units

Units will march through villages at attention, with swords drawn or lances carried. Smart guards will be mounted at Corps, Divisional, Brigade and Regimental H.Q., and trumpet calls will be sounded on the march and in billets as in peace time.

Special care must be taken to leave all billets scrupulously clean, as they will be occupied by the Corps following after.

19. Cavalry Corps H.Q. will move daily with the Divisions. On the 17th it will move to the area SILLY - GONDREGNIES with Report Centre at the MAIRIE, SILLY, and on the 18th to BRAINE LE COMTE with Report Centre at the MAIRIE.

20. Divisional Report Centre as in Order No.82 attached.

15th November, 1918.

Lieut.Colonel,
G.S., 3rd Cavalry Division.

Appendix 11

SECRET.

3rd Cavalry Division Order No. 82.   Copy No. 31

Reference Maps 1/100,000, TOURNAI & BRUSSELS.   15th November, 1918.

1. 3rd Cavalry Division (less Heavy Section Reserve Park) will move on 17th November to Line A (DENDERWINDEKE - ENGHIEN - HORRUES Road) exclusive as shown on attached map issued to Brigades and "Q".

2. Move will take place in accordance with attached March Table.

3. "A" and "B" Echelons, Cavalry Field Ambulances and Mobile Veterinary Sections will accompany Brigades.

4. Heavy Section Reserve Park will remain in present area till further orders.

5. Regulation distances will be maintained.
Brigades may use any roads within their allotted boundaries.

6. 6th Cavalry Brigade will detail one Squadron of 10th Royal Hussars as escort to Corps Commander. This Squadron will join Cavalry Corps H.Q. at the Mairie, SILLY, on November 17th, arriving there not later than 13.00 hours.
The Squadron will be accompanied by its proportion of Horse Transport and M.T.

7. Cavalry Corps H.Q. will move on 17th November to the area SILLY - GONDREGNIES and Report Centre will open at the Mairie, SILLY, at 13.00. The area SILLY - GONDREGNIES will be exclusive to 6th Cavalry Brigade.
On 18th November, Cavalry Corps H.Q. will move to BRAINE LE COMTE.

8. The Division will continue march forward on 18th November to Line No.1 on attached map issued to Brigades and "Q". An early start is probable so that roads may be cleared for the Infantry.

9. Divisional Report Centre will close at ANTOING at 10.00, 17th November, and reopen at BASSILLY CHURCH at same hour.

10. ACKNOWLEDGE.

Issued at 23.00

Lieut.Colonel,
G.S., 3rd Cavalry Division.

Distribution -   List "A", less A.H.T.Company & Divisional Obs.Section, and plus II Corps and 1st Cavalry Division.

March Table issued with 3rd Cavalry Division Order No.82

Serial No.	Date.	Unit.	Starting Point.	Time to pass S.P.	Route.	Destination.	Remarks.
1.	Nov. 17th	6th Cav.Bde.	E. exit of LEUZE.	08.30.	LEUZE - ATH - ATTRE Road (inclusive) and any roads North of this up to and exclusive of FRASNES-LEZ- BUISSENAL - LAHAMAIDE - LESSINES Road.	Area as follows:- East Boundary Line A from HORRUES (excl.) to a point 2 miles N. of ENGHIEN (exl.). South Boundary Dividing line between Divisions. West Boundary FOULENG (incl.) - BRUNFAUT (incl.) - BASSILLY (exclusive) - ROMONT (incl.) North Boundary = ST.PIERRE CAPELLE (incl.).	
2.	17th	7th Cav.Bde.	ELLEZELLES	08.30.	Any roads between ELLEZELLES - FLOBECQ - SOTTENIERE - GHOY - LES DEUX ACREN Road and RENAIX - OPBRAKEL - PARICKE - SCHENDELBEKE Road - both above roads inclusive.	Area as follows:- East Boundary Line A from a point 2 miles N. of ENGHIEN to DENDERWINDEKE (excl.) South Boundary ST. PIERRE CAPELLE (excl.) to BIEVENE (incl.) West Boundary BIEVENE - MOERBEKE - GRAMMONT Road to T of GRAMMONT (Road inclusive) - SCHENDELBEKE (incl.). North Boundary SCHENDELBEKE - SANTBERGEN (both inclusive).	

P.T.O.

Serial No.	Date. NOV.	Unit.	Starting Point.	Time to pass S.P.	Route.	Destination.	Remarks.
3.	17th	Canadian Cav. Bde.	X Roads at B. of BECLERS.	08.30.	THIMOUGIES to HACQUEGNIES; thence any roads between FRASNES LES BUISSENAL - LANANAIDE - LESSINES Road (inclusive) and LEUZE - ATH - ENGHIEN Road (exclusive).	Area as follows:- East Boundary LA CAVEE BIEVENE - MOERBEKE Road (all exclusive). South Boundary BOURLON (exclusive) to Point 62 ½ mile N. of H in HELLEBECQ. West Boundary OLLIGNIES - LESSINES - GRAMMONT Road (all inclusive). North Boundary GRAMMONT Road (inclusive).	
4.	17th	Divl. H.Q. H.Q. F.H.A. H.Q. A.S.C. 3rd Sig.Sqdn.	Road junction ½ mile N. of AM of RAMECROIX.	09.30.	LEUZE - ATH.	BASSILLY.	Order of March as in Column 3.
5.	17th	D. A. C.	Eastern exit of LEUZE.	10.00.	LEUZE - ATH.	BOURLON (1 mile N.W. of BASSILLY).	
6.	17th	3rd Field Squadron (less 2 Troops).	Eastern exit of LEUZE.	10.30.	LEUZE - ATH.	HELLEBECQ.	
7.	17th	Light Sect. Reserve Park.	Eastern exit of LEUZE.	10.45.	LEUZE - ATH.	STOQUOI (2 miles W. of BASSILLY).	

SECRET.

G.S.248/9
17.11.18.

Reference 3rd Cavalry Division Order No. 83.

1. Z Hour will be at 08.30 Hours.

2. Canadian Cavalry Brigade will close up into the Eastern portion of their area and will be East of a line first E of GRAMMONT - N of LES DEUX ACREN - E of BOIS DE LESSINES by 09.00 Hours.

3. Infantry advance will commence at 09.00 Hours daily. Troops of Cavalry Divisions will be well clear of the Western Boundaries of their areas by that hour. It is essential that the Infantry march is not delayed.

4. Reference Serial Nos. 5 & 6, Billeting Parties of Divisional Troops will meet Camp Commandant at X Roads just N.W. of first E of ENGHIEN at 09.45 Hours.

5. ACKNOWLEDGE.

17th November, 1918.

Lieut.Colonel,
G.S., 3rd Cavalry Division.

DISTRIBUTION - All recipients of 3rd Cav. Div. Order No. 83.

Appendix 12

SECRET.

3rd Cavalry Division Order No.83.   Copy No.....

Reference 1/100,000 Sheets TOURNAI & BRUSSELS.   November 16th, 1918.

1.   3rd Cavalry Division (less Heavy Section Reserve Park) will continue the march on November 18th to "LINE 1" as shewn on map issued to Brigades with Order No.82.
     March Table attached.

2.   Hour of start (Z Hour) will be notified later.

3.   "A" and "B" Echelons, Cavalry Field Ambulances and Mobile Veterinary Sections will accompany Brigades.

4.   Troops may march closed up but 50 yards distance should be left between Squadrons and similar units, and 50 yards between groups of 12 vehicles.

5.   Dividing line between leading Brigades:-
     Point where railway crossed "LINE 1" 1½ miles W. of HAL - RUE AU BOIS (inclusive to 7th Cavalry Brigade) - Point 2 miles N. of ENGHIEN on ENGHIEN - DENDERWINDEKE Road.
     Leading Brigades (6th and 7th) may use any roads within allotted boundaries.

6.   Divisional Report Centre will close at BASSILLY at 11.00 on 18th instant and re-open at ENGHIEN (Cross Roads just N.W. of 1st E of ENGHIEN) at the same hour.

7.   ACKNOWLEDGE.

                                            [signature]
                                                Lieut.Colonel,
                                        G.S., 3rd Cavalry Division.
Issued at 18.00.
----
                                    3 Can Res Par
Distribution - List "A" less A.H.T. Company and O.C.Div.Obs.Section,
               and plus   1st Cavalry Division.

March Order issued with 3rd Cavalry Division Order No.83.

Serial No.	Date NOV.	Unit.	Starting Point.	Time to pass S.P.	Route.	Destination.	Remarks.
1.	18th	6th Cavalry Brigade.	Under Brigade arrangements.	Z Hour.	Any within allotted boundaries.	Area as follows:— East Boundary:- "LINE 1" from Dividing Line between Divisions to point where railway crosses "LINE 1" 1½ miles W. of HAL. South Boundary- Dividing Line between Divisions. West Boundary - SENNE River to REBECQ ROGNON (exclusive) thence CROLY - BIERGHES - LEPINE all inclusive. North Boundary - Dividing line between Brigades.	
2.	18th	7th Cavalry Brigade.	Under Brigade arrangements.	Z Hour.	Any within allotted Boundaries.	Area as follows:— East Boundary- "LINE 1" from Dividing line between Brigades to Northern Div. Boundary. South Boundary - Dividing line between Brigades. West Boundary - RUE AU BOIS (excl. for billeting) — HAUTECROIX - CASTRE — OETINGHEN - DENDERWINDEKE all inclusive. North Boundary - Northern Divisional Boundary.	

P.T.O.

Serial No.	Date. Nov.	Unit.	Starting Point.	Time to pass S.P.	Route.	Distinction.	Remarks.
3.	18th	Canadian Cavalry Bde.	Under Brigade arrangements.	Z+30 mins.	Any Roads excluding BASSILLY - ENGHIEN - HOVES Road.	Area as follows:- East Boundary - Western boundary of 6th and 7th Cav. Bdes. South Boundary - SENNE River from REBECQ ROGNON inclusive to Line A. West Boundary - Line A to VELLEZEEL (inclusive). North Boundary - OETINGHEM - CASTRE (both exclusive).	NOTE: (i) The area ENGHIEN - PETIT ENGHIEN - COQUAINE - STEENKUP is reserved for Divl. H.Q. and Divl. Troops and is exclusive to Canadian Cav.Bde. (ii) Canadian Cav. Bde. will close up towards Eastern portion of Brigade area before hour of starting to clear way for Infantry advance.
4.	18th	Divl. H.Q. H.C. R.H.A. H.Q. A.S.C. 3rd Signal Squadron.	INN near 38th mile-stone on BASSILLY - ENGHIEN Road.	Z Hour.	BASSILLY - ENGHIEN.	ENGHIEN.	Order of march as in Column 3.
5.	18th	D.A.C.	do.	Z+30 mins.	do.	ENGHIEN.	Billets from Camp Commandant.
6.	18th	3rd Field Egdn.(less 2 Troops).	do.	Z+1 hour.	do.	ENGHIEN.	Billets from Camp Commandant.
7.	18th	Light Sect. Reserve Pk.	do.	Z+1½ hours.	do.	PETIT ENGHIEN.	

Appendix 13

3RD. CAVALRY DIVISION ORDER NO. 84.

SECRET.

Copy No. 25

Reference 1/100,000 Sheets issued
with 3rd Cav. Div. Order No. 82.

19th. November, 1918.

1. 3rd Cavalry Division will continue the march on November 21st to the general line GEMBLOUX - WAVRE Road - OTTENBOURG (inclusive).
Move will take place in accordance with March Table attached.

2. Canadian Cavalry Brigade will relieve 7th Cavalry Brigade as left advanced Brigade. It will pass through 7th Cavalry Brigade at commencement of march and come into position on left of 6th Cavalry Brigade, in accordance with March Table.
Details as regards taking over dispositions will be arranged direct between G.Os.C. Brigades concerned.

3. The Field Troop R.E. and Pack Wireless Detachment now attached to 7th Cavalry Brigade will be taken over by Canadian Cavalry Brigade under arrangements between Brigades direct.
Similarly 7th Cavalry Brigade will take over Section R.E. now attached to Canadian Cavalry Brigade.

4. Dividing line between leading Brigades:-
Kilometre 27 (1,000 yards S. of WAVRE) - RIXENSART - GENVAL (both inclusive to Canadian Cavalry Brigade) - WATERLOO (exclusive to Canadian Cavalry Brigade) - TOURNEPIE (inclusive to Canadian Cavalry Brigade) - Point where HAL - ENGHIEN Railway crosses "Line 1".

5. (a) Troops may march closed up, but intervals should be left as stated in para. 4 of 3rd Cavalry Division Order No. 83.

(b) Rate of advance:- 5 miles per hour.

6. "A" and "B" Echelons, Cavalry Field Ambulances and Mobile Veterinary Sections accompany Brigades and units of Divisional Troops.

7. The march will be continued on November 22nd to the general line PONTILLAS (exclusive) - FORVILLE (exclusive) - HEMPTINNE - BRANCHON (both inclusive) - JAUCHE (exclusive).
Hour of start will be 09.00 hours.

8. Divisional Report Centre will close at ENGHIEN at 11.00 hours on November 21st and re-open at WATERLOO (X Roads N. end of Village) at the same hour.

9. ACKNOWLEDGE.

Issued at 18.00 hours.

Lieut.Colonel,
G.S., 3rd Cavalry Division.

Distribution - List "A", less 3rd Cav. Reserve Park, Aux. H.T.Company and
O.C. Div.Obs. Section, and plus 1st Cavalry Divn., 29th
Divn., 41st Divn., Belgian Mission and II Corps, and
Light Section 3rd Cav. Res. Park.

March Table issued with 3rd Cavalry Division Order No. 84.

Serial No.	Date. NOV.	Unit.	Starting Point.	Time to pass S.P.	Route.	Destination.	Remarks.
1.	21st.	6th Cavalry Brigade.	Under Brigade arrangements.	08.30.	Any within allotted boundaries except the main STEHOUX - HAL Road.	Area as follows:- East Boundary: GEMBLOUX - WAVRE Road to Kilometre 27. South Boundary: Dividing line between Divisions. West Boundary: W of WANROUX - A of COUTURE St.GERMAIN - Chaple St. LAMBERT inclusive. North Boundary: Dividing line between Brigades.	6th Cav. Bde. to give precedence to Canadian Regt. (R.C.D.) moving along STEHOUX - HAL Road.
2.	21st.	Canadian Cavalry Brigade.	do.	Heads of Columns to cross "Line 1" at 08.30 and Bde. to be clear of that line by 09.15.	Any within allotted boundaries.	Area as follows:- East Boundary Kilometre 27 on GEMBLOUX - WAVRE Road - WAVRE inclusive - OTTENBOURG inclusive - SMOISBERG inclusive. South Boundary: Dividing line between Brigades. West Boundary: GENVAL - LA HULPE - HOEYLAERT all inclusive. North Boundary: Northern Divisional Boundary.	Regiment at REBECQ. ROGNON may use main SAINTES - HAL Road but must proceed to it by road running through E of WISBECQ - H of BIERGHES.

Serial No.	Date. NOV.	Unit.	Starting Point.	Time to pass S.P.	Route.	Destination.	Remarks.
3.	21st.	7th Cavalry Brigade.	Under Brigade arrangements.	Heads of Columns to cross "Line 1" at 09.30 and any roads South of this & Bde. to be clear of that line by 10.30 hours.	LEERBEEK - HAL - ALSEMBERG - BRAINE L'ALLEUD - SAINTES - TUBIZE - BRAINE-LE-CHATEAU - WATERLOO Road.	Area as follows:- East Boundary: Western boundaries of 6th and Canadian Cav. Bdes. South Boundary:Dividing line between Divisions. West Boundary: GLABAIS - BRAINE L'ALLEUD - ALSEMBURG all exclusive. North Boundary: RHODE ST. GENESE (incl.) to Kilometre 11 on W. edge of SOIGNIES Forest - HOEYLAERT(exclusive).	(i) 7th Cav. Bde. will close up their tail from the DENDERWINDEKE - OETINGHEM portion of their area so that it is on the line of NEYGHEM - LEERBEEK Road by 09.00. (ii) 7th Cav.Bde. to be clear of X Roads 1½ miles N. of BRAINE l'ALLEUD by 13.30 hours.
4.	21st.	Divl. P.Q. H.Q. R.H.A. H.Q. A.S.C. 3rd Sig.Sqdn.	Road junction between Kilometres 25 & 26 on main ENGHIEN - HAL Road.	09.00.	SAINTES - TUBIZE - BRAINE LE CHATEAU - X Roads 1½ miles N. of BRAINE L'ALLEUD.	WATERLOO.	
5.	21st.	3rd Field Sqdn. less 2 Troops.	do.	09.10.	do.	WATERLOO.	Billets from Camp Commandant.
6.	21st.	D.A.C.	do.	09.15.	do.	ROUSSART & JOLIBOIS.	
7.	21st.	Light Sect. Reserve Park.	do.	09.35.	do.	MONT ST. JEAN.	

Appendix 14

SECRET.

3rd Cavalry Division Order No. 85.   Copy No. 24

Reference 1/100,000 Sheets issued
with 3rd Cav. Div. Order No. 82.   20th November, 1918.

1. 3rd Cavalry Division will continue the march on November 22nd to the general line P of PONTILLAS - FORVILLE (exclusive) - HEMPTINNE - BRANCHON (both inclusive) - JAUCHE (exclusive).

2. Dividing line between leading Brigades Point 152 1½ miles North of HEMPTINNE - BONEFFE - THOREMBAIX-LES-BEGUINES - CHAUMONT-GISTOUX - GISTOUX - DION-LE-MONT (all inclusive to Canadian Cavalry Brigade) - Kilo. 27 on WAVRE - GEMBLOUX Road.

3. Echelons, Cavalry Field Ambulances and Mobile Veterinary Sections accompany Brigades.

4. Rate of march - 5 miles per hour.

5. Divisional Report Centre will close at WATERLOO at 11.00 on November 22nd and re-open at PERWEZ at same hour.

6. ACKNOWLEDGE.

Issued at 18.30.

                                      Lieut. Colonel,
                              G.S., 3rd Cavalry Division.

Distribution - List "A", less 3rd Cav. Reserve Park, Aux. H.T.Company
               and O.C. Div. Obs.Section, and plus Light Section
               Reserve Park, 1st Cavalry Divn., 29th Divn., 41st Divn.,
               Belgian Mission and II Corps.

March Table issued with 3rd Cavalry Division Order No.85.

Serial No.	Date. NOV.	Unit.	Starting Point.	Time to pass S.P.	Route.	Destination.	Remarks.
1.	22nd.	6th Cavalry Bde.	Under Brigade arrangements.	09.00.	Any within Brigade Boundaries.	Area as follows:- East Boundary: PONTILLAS - FORVILLE (both excl.) - HEMPTINNE (inclusive). North Boundary: Dividing line between Brigades. West Boundary: LA GRAND ROSIERE (inclusive) - JAUSSELETTE (exclusive) - BARAQUE (incl.). South Boundary: Divisional Dividing Line.	
2.	22nd.	Canadian Cavalry Brigade.	do.	09.00.	do.	Area as follows:- East Boundary: BRANCHON (incl.) - JANDRENOUILLE - JAUCHE (both exclusive). North Boundary: Northern Divisional Boundary. West Boundary: ST.JOSSE (excl.) - JAUCHELETTE - GLIMES (both exclusive.), thence main road GLIMES - GRAND ROSIERE. South Boundary: Brigade Dividing Line.	

P. T. O.

-2-

Serial No.	Date. NOV.	Unit.	Starting Point.	Time to Pass S.P.	Route.	Destination.	Remarks.
3.	22nd.	7th Cavalry Bde.	Under Brigade arrangements	09.00.	Any, (except GENVAL – ROSIERES – WAVRE – PERWEZ).	Area as follows:— East Boundary: Western boundary of Canadian Cavalry Bde. North Boundary: Northern Divisional Boundary. West Boundary: SART MELIN – ROUX MIROIR – SART RISBART – STE. MARIE WASTINES – ORBAIS (all exclusive) South Boundary: Railway line from GEMBLOUX to GEEST-GEROMPONT.	
4.	22nd.	Divl. H.Q. H.Q. R.H.A. H.Q. A.S.C. 3rd Sig.Sqdn.	HANONSART.	09.00.	GENVAL – ROSIERES – WAVRE – PERWEZ.	PERWEZ.	
5.	22nd.	3rd Field Squadron(less 2 Troops).	do.	09.05.	As for Serial No. 4.	PERWEZ.	Billets from Camp Commdt.
6.	22nd.	D. A. C.	do.	09.10.	do. do.	LE MONT.	
7.	22nd.	Light Sect. Reserve Park.	do.	09.30.	do. do.	JAUSELETTE.	

Appendix 15

SECRET.

3rd Cavalry Division Order No. 86.   Copy No...27...

23rd November, 1918.

1. 3rd Cavalry Division area will be readjusted tomorrow, November 24th, as under.

2. No troops (except billeting parties) will cross boundary between 1st and 3rd Cavalry Divisions before 12 Noon.

3. (a) Divisional H.Q.)
       H.Q. A.S.C.   ) ... to MALEVES STE.MARIE WASTINES.
       3rd Signal Squadron.)

   To start at 12 Noon. Any route.

   (b) H.Q. 4th Bde. R.H.A.)
       3rd Field Squadron (less 2 Troops)) ... to THOREMBAIS ST.TROND.
       Light Sect., 3rd Cav.Reserve Park.)

   To start at 12 Noon. Any route.

   Billeting representatives to meet Adjutant R.H.A. who will allot billets at Church at THOREMBAIS ST. TROND at 10.30.

   (c) 6th Cavalry Brigade - to area LIERNU - ST. GERMAIN - DHUY - HARRISOULX - DAUSSOULX - VEDRIN - LES ROSTAILLES - EHION - UPIGNY.
       To clear present billets by 13.00 Hours. Any Route.
       To give precedence to 1st Cavalry Division on road.

   (d) 7th Cavalry Brigade - to area MAISON DU BOIS - SART MELIN - HAPPEAU - INCOURT - OPREBRAIS - WASTINES - THOREMB.ISOUL - GLIMES - JAUCHELETTE - BRUYERE - JODOIGNE SOUVERAINE - HUSSOMPONT - MELIN.
       To clear villages now occupied outside above area by 13.00 hours. Any route.

   (e) Canadian Cavalry Brigade - to area THOREMBAIS - LES - BEGUINES - PERWEZ (exluding LEMONT) - BARAQUE - AISCHE-en-REFAIL - MEHAIGNE - TOMBOIS exclusive - MONT ST.ANDRE - ROMAL.
       To clear present billets by 13.00 hours. Any Route, but not to enter THOREMBAIS LES BEGUINES - PERWEZ - JAUSSELETTE - AISCHE-en-REFAIL and MEHAIGNE before 13.00 hours.

   (f) D.A.C. remain at LEMONT.

4. Divisional H.Q. will close at PERWEZ at 14.00 hours and reopen at MALEVES STE.MARIE WASTINES at same hour.

5. ACKNOWLEDGE.

                                            [signature] Major,
                                            G.S., 3rd Cavalry Division.

Issued at 20.30.

Distribution - List A less 3rd Cav.Res.Park, A.E.T.Coy., Obs. Section, and plus Light Section Reserve Park, French Mission, Belgian Mission, 1st Cavalry Division, II Corps, 9th Divn., 29th Divn., 41st Divn.

Appendix 16

SECRET.

3rd Cavalry Division Order No.87.   Copy No. 9....

30th November, 1918.

1. Following moves will take place tomorrow, December 1st. :-

   3rd Field Squadron R.E. to TOURINNES ST. LAMBERT.

   Field Troop R.E. now attached Canadian Cavalry Brigade to TOURINNES ST.LAMBERT, to rejoin 3rd Field Squadron on arrival.

   Field Troop R.E. now attached 6th Cavalry Brigade to TOURINNES ST. LAMBERT, to rejoin 3rd Field Squadron on arrival.

   Brigades will issue necessary orders for the move of their Field Squadron detachments. Moves to be completed by 16.00 hours.

2. Following villages are allotted to Brigades as additional billeting accommodation:-

6th Cavalry Brigade	...	LEUZE and MEUX.
7th do. do.	...	AUTRE EGLISE.
Canadian Cavalry Bde.	...	ORBAIS - GRANDE ROSIERE - GEEST GERAMPONT - NOVILLE SUR MEHAIGNE.

   Brigades will inform this Office by December 1st if they do not propose making use of above area.

3. ACKNOWLEDGE.

                                    Shore   Major,
                              G.S., 3rd Cavalry Division.

Issued at 12.30.

Distribution - List "A" less 3rd Cav. Res. Park, A.H.T.Coy., O.C.Div. Obs.Section, and plus Light Section Reserve Park.

Confidential

War Diary

of

General Staff.

3rd Cavalry Division.

Intelligence

December, 1918.

Appendix 1.

6th Cavalry Bde.	A.D.M.S.	Aux. H.T.Coy.
7th Cavalry Bde.	A.D.V.S.	"Q"
Canadian Cav. Bde.	A.P.M.	Camp Commandant.
3rd Signal Squadron.	O.C. A.S.C.	
3rd Field Squadron R.E.	3rd Cav.Res.Pk.	
C.R.H.A.	D.A.C.	

G.S.210/70.
6.12.18.

3rd Cavalry Division will be prepared to move on December 9th and 10th from present area to winter area. Further detailed orders will be issued later.

6th December, 1918.

[signature] Major,
G.S., 3rd Cavalry Division.

"A" Form — Army Form C. 2121 (In pads of 100.)
MESSAGES AND SIGNALS.

Appendix 2

| TO | All concerned. | | |

Sender's Number.	Day of Month.	In reply to Number.	
G.758	7th		AAA

Cancel G.S.210/70 of 6th AAA Division will not move before Dec. 14th into permanent winter area AAA Further definite orders follow tomorrow.

From 3rd Cavalry Division.
Place
Time 08.00

(Z) (Sd) S.G.HOWES, Major.

Appendix 2

			SECRET.
6th Cav. Bde.	D.A.C.	O.C. A.S.C.	
7th Cav. Bde.	"Q".	Light Sect.Reserve Park.	
Canadian Cav.Bde.	A.D.M.S.	Aux. H.T. Coy.	
3rd Signal Squadron.	A.D.V.S.	Cavalry Corps.	
3rd Field Squadron R.E.	D.A.P.M.		
C.R.H.A.	Camp Comdt.		

G.S.210/71.
7.12.18.

All previous orders regarding move to permanent winter area are cancelled.

6th Cavalry Brigade will march on December 10th to a staging area HUY (exclusive) - ANTHIET (inclusive) - VINALMONT (inclusive) - FUMAL (inclusive) - HUCCORGNE - MOHA - BAS OHA (all inclusive).

This Brigade will halt there on December 11th and will march on December 12th to their permanent winter area (Area A as marked on maps given to Brigades), with the exception that the Valley of the MEUSE on both banks of the river will not be available for billeting until December 16th. Area B, less Valley of the MEUSE, will also be available for this Brigade to billet in until December 16th if required.

Detailed orders regarding march of 6th Cavalry Brigade on December 10th and 12th will be issued later.

2. Remainder of Division will probably march on December 15th and stage night 15/16th on the western boundary of permanent winter area, moving into permanent winter area on December 16th.

3. ACKNOWLEDGE.

7th December, 1918.

Major,
G.S., 3rd Cavalry Division.

Appendix 3

SECRET.

3rd Cavalry Division Order No.88.

Copy No.... 20

Reference Maps 1/100,000.
BRUSSELS, NAMUR, LIEGE, MARCHE.

9th December, 1918.

1.   In continuation of G.S.210/71 dated 7.12.18, 6th Cavalry Brigade complete with A and B Echelons will march on December 10th to a staging area HUY (exclusive) - ANTHIET - VINALMONT - FUMAL - HUCCORGNE - MOHA - BAS OHA (all inclusive).

2.   6th Cavalry Brigade will halt on December 11th.

3.   On December 12th, 6th Cavalry Brigade will march to their permanent winter area (Area A) less Valley of the MEUSE.
     Area B less Valley of MEUSE is available for billeting this Brigade if required until December 16th.

4.   No restrictions as to roads.

5.   Remainder of the Division will move on 15th December, staging night 15/16th in an area to be notified later.

6.   R.C.H.A. Brigade Ammunition Column will join R.C.H.A. Brigade on December 15th, moving from present area under orders of Canadian Cavalry Brigade. It will be billeted by R.C.H.A. Brigade in permanent winter area and will form part of R.C.H.A. Brigade until further orders.

7.   Attention is drawn to following moves which will be taking place through Cavalry Corps area.

   (a) The tail of the IX Corps will be clear of the line of the OURTHE River on the 12th, and of the frontier on the 15th instant.

   (b) The New Zealand Division will be marching through parts of the Cavalry Corps area as follows:-
     On 15th its head will be at SERAING, its tail at HUY.
     " 16th "   "   "   " " FRAIPONT, "   "   " SERAING.
     " 17th)
       and "   "   "   " " VERVIERS, "   "   " FRAIPONT.
       18th)
     " 19th "   "   "   " " ROTTGEN,   "   "   " VERVIERS.

8.   ACKNOWLEDGE.

Issued at 18.00 hrs.

[signed] Major,
G.S., 3rd Cavalry Division.

Distribution - List A.

Appendix 4

SECRET.

3rd Cavalry Division Order No. 89.   Copy No. 25

Reference Maps 1/100,000 BRUSSELS, NAMUR, LIEGE & MARCHE.   12th Dec. 1918.

1.   3rd Cavalry Division (less 6th Cavalry Brigade) will move to a Staging Area on 15th December and to permanent area on 16th December, in accordance with March Tables attached.

2.   A and B Echelons will accompany Brigades.

3.   Distances as laid down in S.S.724 will be maintained.

4.   Divisional Report Centre will close at MALEVES STE. MARIE WASTINES at 11.00 hours on 16th December and re-open at SOHEIT TINLOT at same hour.

5.   Any troops of 6th Cavalry Brigade now billeted in Area B will be North of River MEUSE by 09.00 hours on 16th instant

6.   ACKNOWLEDGE.

                                        Swire Capt
                                            for
                                        Major,
                                G.S., 3rd Cavalry Division.

Issued at
18.00

Addressed List "A".

March Table "A" issued with 3rd Cavalry Division Order No.89.

Serial No.	Date.	Unit.	Starting Point.	Time.	Route.	Destination.	Remarks.
1.	Dec. 15th.	7th Cav. Bde.	Any.	---	Any Roads N. of GRAND ROSIERE - EGHEZEE - HUY main road.	Area N. of LIEGE - NAMUR Railway - WANZE - MOHA - HUCCORGNE - FUMAL - VILLERS LE BOUILLET (all incl.) - AMPSIN (excl.).	Fighting troops and A Echelon to be East of HANNUT - BIERWART - NAMUR Road by 12.30.
2.	15th.	Canadian Cav. Bde.+R.C.H.A Bde.Ammn.Col.	Road junction at EGHEZEE.	11.00	FORVILLE - BIERWART.	Area N. of River MEUSE - LES HOUILLERES - VE AINE - FORSEILLES - HERON - BURDINNE - OTEPPE - MARNEFFE - LONGPRE (all incl.) - BAS OHA (excl.).	
3.	15th.	D.A.C.	As for Serial No. 2.	12.30	ditto.	WARET L'EVEQUE - HALBOSEL.	Billets from Camp Commandant.
4.	15th.	H.Q. R.H.A. Divl. H.Q. Details. 3rd Sig.Sqdn. H.Q. R.A.S.C. & A.H.T.Coy.	PERWEZ STATION.	11.00	GRAND ROSIERE - EGHEZEE - FORVILLE.	WARET L'EVEQUE. H.Q. R.A.S.C. & A.H.T. Coy. to BIERWART.	In order of march as stated in Column 3.
5.	15th.	3rd Field Squadron.	As for Serial No. 4.	11.15	ditto.	BAS OHA & OHA.	
6.	15th.	Light Sect. 3rd Cav.Res. Park.	As for Serial No. 4.	11.30	ditto.	BIERWART & OTREPPE.	

March Table "B" issued with 3rd. Cavalry Division Order No. 89.

Serial No.	Date.	Unit.	Starting Point.	Time.	Route.	Destination.	Remarks.
1.	Dec. 16th.	7th Cav. Bde.	Any.	—	Any, but only Bridges at HUY and AMAY to be used.	Area C.	To be East of a grid line N. and S. through H of HUY by 10.00.
2.	16th.	3rd Field Sqdn.	Fork Roads at 2nd Kilostone ½ mile S.E. of E of WANZE.	10.00	Any, but to cross at AMAY.	TILFF.	
3.	16th.	Canadian Cav. Bde.+ R.C.H.A. Bde.Amm.Col.	As for Serial No. 2.	10.15.	As for Serial No. 1.	Area B.	
4.	16th.	Divl. H.Q. Details. 3rd Sig.Sqdn. H.Q. R.A.S.C.& H.Q. A.H.T.Co. H.Q. R.H.A.	LAVOIR.	10.45	WANZE - HUY Bridge.	Divl.H.Q., Signal Sqdn., H.Q.A.S.C. to SOHEIT TINLOT - FRAITURE area. H.Q. R.H.A. to ST.VITU area 1¾ miles East of STREE.	In order of march as stated in Column 3.
5.	16th.	D. A. C.	As for Serial No. 4.	11.00	As for Serial No. 4.	ABEE.	
6.	16th.	Light Sect. 3rd Cav.Res. Park.	As for Serial No. 4.	11.15	As for Serial No. 4.	TERWAGNE - LINEHET area.	

Appendix 5.

SECRET

Amendment to 3rd Cavalry Division Order No.89.

1. Reference 3rd Cavalry Division Order No.89, the Commander-in-Chief will inspect the Canadian Cavalry Brigade tomorrow, December 15th, as they march from the present area to staging area.

2. The Commander-in-Chief will be at the fork roads just North of the H of HALBOSEL (½ mile S.E. of BIERWART) at 12.50.

3. At 12.30 the head of the Canadian Cavalry Brigade will be halted just West of these fork roads at the H of HALBOSEL. The column will be closed up.

4. The Acting Brigadier of Canadian Cavalry Brigade will meet the Commander-in-Chief at the fork roads at the H of HALBOSEL at 12.45.

5. In consequence of the above, the amended March Table "A", issued with 3rd Cavalry Division Order No.89, will be further amended as follows:-

   Serial No.2.   Amend time to pass starting point to read "11.00".
   "   " 3.   "   "   "   "   "   "   "   "   "12.30".
   "   " 4.   Amend route for 3rd Field Squadron to read:
                  "Any road North of Gd. ROSIERE - EGHEZEE - HUY main road".
   "   " 5.   Amend time to pass starting point to read "11.30".
   "   " 6.   "   "   "   "   "   "   "   "   "11.45".
   "   " 7.   "   "   "   "   "   "   "   "   "12.00".

6. ACKNOWLEDGE.

14th December, 1918.

[signature] Major,
G.S., 3rd Cavalry Division.

Addressed List "A" plus Fourth Army.

Appendix 6

SECRET

Amendment No.1 to 3rd Cavalry Division Order No.89
dated 12th December, 1918.

The March Tables "A" and "B" issued with 3rd Cavalry Division Order No.89, dated 12th December 1918, are cancelled, and the attached Tables "A" and "B" substituted.

                                                                       Major.

14th December, 1918.   G.S., 3rd Cavalry Division.

List A, plus
       2nd Cavalry Division.
       New Zealand Division.
       Fourth Army.

Amended. March Table 'A' issued with 3rd. Cav. Div. Order No. 89.

Serial No.	Date	Unit	Starting Point	Time to pass starting point	Route	Destination	Remarks
1.	15th.	7th. Cav. Bde.	Any.	—	Any roads N. of GRAND ROSIERE – EGHEZEE – HUY main road.	WALEFFE, CHAPON SERAING – FUMAL (incl) MARNEFFE (excl) OTEPPE – BURDINNE – MOXHE – AVENNES (all incl) LES WALEFFES (excl).	
2.	15th.	Can.Cav. Bde. & R.C.H.A.Bde Ammn. Col.	Road junction at EGHEZEE.	10.00	FORVILLE – BIERWART.	MARNEFFE – LONGPRE – JAVA (all excl) Southern boundary River MEUSE – Northern boundary OTEPPE – BURDINNE (both excl) No limit to Western boundary.	BIERWART – OTREPPE – WARET L'EVEQUE – HAL BOSEL exclusive to Can.Bde.
3.	15th.	D.A.C.	– do –	11.30	– do –	WARET L'EVEQUE.	
4.	15th.	3rd. Fd. Sqdn.	PERWEZ Stn.	10.00	Any.	BORLEZ & AINEFFE.	
5.	15th.	H.Q. R.H.A. 3rd. Signal Sqdn.	– do –	10.15	GRAND ROSIERE – ECHEZEE – FORVILLE	WARET L'EVEQUE.	
6.	15th.	Div.H.Q.Details H.Q. R.A.S.C. & H.Q. A.H.T.Coy.	– do –	10.30	– do –	BIERWART.	
7.	15th.	Light Sect. 3rd. Cav. Res. Park.	– do –	10.45	– do –	BIERWART.	

Amended March Table "B" issued with 3rd Cavalry Division Order No.89.

Serial No.	Date. DEC.	Unit.	Starting Point.	Time to pass S.P.	Route.	Destination.	Remarks.
1.	16th	7th Cavalry Bde.	Any.	---	Any. To cross R. MEUSE by any bridges between HUY (incl.) and SERAING (excl.)	Area C.	Columns crossing at HUY & AMAY to be S. of R. MEUSE by 10.30.
2.	16th	Canadian Cav.Bde. + R.C.H.A.Bde. Ammn. Column.	Fork roads at 2nd Kilo. stone ½ mile S.E. of E of WANZE.	10.00	Ditto.	Area "B"	
3.	16th	3rd Field Sqdr.	Any.	---	Any, but to cross MEUSE at ENGIS.	TILFF.	Not to cross MEUSE before 10.30 hours.
4.	16th	H.Q. R.H.A. 3rd Signal Sqdn. Divl. H.Q.Details H.Q. R.A.S.C. & H.Q. A.H.T.Coy.	LAVOIR.	10.45.	WANZE - HUY Bridge.	Divl.H.Q. Signal Sqdn., H.Q.R.A.S.C. march as in to SOHEIT TINLOT-FRAITURE area. H.Q. R.H.A. to ST. VITU area 1½ miles East of STREE.	In order of march as in Column 3.
5.	16th	D.A.C.	LAVOIR.	11.00	Ditto.	ABEE.	
6.	16th	Light Section, 3rd Cav.Res.Pk.	LAVOIR.	11.15.	Ditto.	TERWAGNE - LIBERT Area.	

6th Cavalry Brigade.	D.A.C.	SECRET.
7th Cavalry Brigade.	O.C. R.A.S.C.	
Canadian Cav.Bde.	A.D.M.S.	
3rd Signal Squadron.	D.A.P.M.	G.S.248/97
3rd Field Sqdn.R.E.	Camp Commdt.	21.12.18.
C.R.H.A.	"Q".	

----

1. Cavalry Corps have been ordered to vacate a portion on the Northern Boundary of their area, and the new boundary of the 3rd Cavalry Division area is shewn on attached map marked in blue ink (attached for Brigades only).

2. In order to compensate for the area lost, the Division has been allowed to extend Southwards into unallotted area as follows:-

   Eastern Boundary from S.E. corner of present area HAMOIR (incl.) - thence due South to BOMAL (incl.) - BARVAUX (incl.) - EREZEE (incl.).

   Southern Boundary from EREZEE - HOTTON (incl.) - Eastern Boundary of X Corps area just South of BAILLONVILLE (incl.).

   Western Boundary - The Eastern Boundary of X Corps area, i.e. South to North BAILLONVILLE(incl.) - MAFFE (excl.) - LES AVINS (excl.) - MODAVE (incl.) - PONT DE BONNE (excl.) - O in JOUETTE (just West of AMPSIN) - FIZE FONTAINE (incl.) - CHAPON SERAING (excl.) - VIEMME (excl.).

3. The areas tentatively allotted to Brigades and Divisional Troops are marked in Red, but are subject to alteration after reconnaissances have been carried out by Brigades.

4. 7th and Canadian Cavalry Brigades will therefore reconnoitre their areas forthwith and will forward a marked map to Divisional H.Q. as soon as possible but not later than 28th instant, shewing how they propose to allot their areas.

5. Brigade areas are subject to the following restrictions:-

   6th Cavalry Brigade area - AMPSIN is not to be used for billeting without reference to 3rd Cavalry Division "Q".

   7th Cavalry Brigade area - 7th Cavalry Brigade will be prepared to accommodate an Army Troops Coy. R.E., strength 140 all ranks and 25 horses, in their area, on or near the TERWAGNE - MARCHE Road. (BOIS-et-BORSU is suggested).

6. (a) Cavalry Corps are negotiating with Belgian authorities for 3rd Field Squadron to be allowed to remain in SCHLESSIN.

   (b) A new area is required for D.A.C.
   O.C. D.A.C. will reconnoitre MODAVE at once and will report result of reconnaissance to Divisional H.Q. by 23rd inst.

   (c) NANDRIN is added to Divisional H.Q. troops area.

7. Units of Divisional Troops can see a marked map in "G" Office, shewing boundary of whole Divisional Area.
   This map and those attached for Brigades cancel all other maps of Divisional area previously issued.

8. The necessary readjustments in the areas have to be completed by 11.59 hours, December 31st.

21st December, 1918.

(Sd) S.G.HOWES, Major,
G.S., 3rd Cavalry Division.

App. 40

SECRET.

Copy No. 22

3rd Cavalry Division Order No. 42.

Reference 1/100,000 Sheet 17 AMIENS.   15th August, 1918.

1. In continuation of G.X.200/26 dated 15th August, the Division will march during the night 15th/16th August in accordance with March Table overleaf. Troops to be in Camp by 4.30 a.m. 16th.

2. "A" and "B" Echelons will accompany Brigades.

3. Distances laid down in Fourth Army Orders to be maintained from Starting Point.

4. Divisional Report Centre will close at SAINS EN AMIENOIS at 7 P.M. and re-open at YZEUX Chateau at the same hour.

5. Railhead 16th AMIENS (Main Station), 17th HANGEST.

6. ACKNOWLEDGE.

Lieut.Colonel,
G.S., 3rd Cavalry Division.

Issued at 1 P.M.

Copy No.
1 to 6th Cav. Brigade.
2 " 7th " "
3 " Canadian Cav. Bde.
4 " 3rd Signal Sqdn.
5 " 3rd Field Squadron.
6 " C.R.H.A.
7 " D.M.G.O.
8 " "Q"
9 " D.A.C.
10 " 3rd Cav. Reserve Park.
11 " Aux. H.T. Company.
12 " A.D.M.S.
13 " A.D.V.S.
14 " A.P.M.
15 " O.C. A.S.C.
16 " Camp Commandant.

www.ingramcontent.com/pod-product-compliance
Lightning Source LLC
Chambersburg PA
CBHW081527160426
43191CB00011B/1704